# Praise for *You Are My Sunshine*

Sean Dietrich's sentences are the crack cocaine of literary humor. *You Are My Sunshine* is delivered with a style that would make Mark Twain jealous. Trust me: if you liked Lewis Grizzard, you will love Sean Dietrich!

—Andy Andrews, *New York Times* bestselling author of *The Traveler's Gift*, founder of WisdomHarbour.com

A perfect collision of southern wit and tissue-reaching truths. Sean and Jamie's story is authentic, raw, and inspiring. A must-read.

—Laura Jean Bell, host of *Y'all Podcast*

This book is more than a travel guide for the C&O trail. With his characteristic humor, insight, and talent, Sean shows us what it means to keep going . . . through a cancer diagnosis, during a global pandemic, or just over the ridge in the next difficult climb.

—Shawn Smucker, author of *The Weight of Memory*

Sean Dietrich is one of America's greatest living storytellers. His writing is full of heart, humor, and honesty. The world would be a better place if more people read Sean Dietrich's books. That's a fact. Thank the good Lord that Sean Dietrich writes a lot better than he looks. How he landed a woman like Jamie, I'll never know. Sean Dietrich has a gift for storytelling that makes me slightly envious. If I weren't so much better looking than Sean Dietrich, I'd be jealous of how well he writes.

—Christopher Thomas, founder of MADE SOUTH

You Are My Sunshine

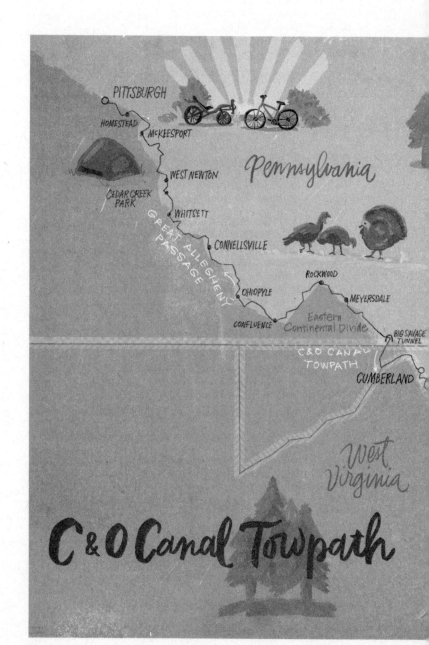

# great Allegheny Passage

Mason & Dixon Line

HANCOCK

LITTLE ORLEANS

WILLIAMSPORT

**Maryland**

PAW PAW

SHEPHERDSTOWN

HARPERS FERRY

BRUNSWICK

LEESBURG

**Virginia**

SENECA CREEK

WASHINGTON, DC

# You Are My Sunshine

### A story of love, promises, and a really long bike ride

## Sean Dietrich

### SEAN OF THE SOUTH

ZONDERVAN
BOOKS

ZONDERVAN BOOKS

*You Are My Sunshine*
Copyright © 2022 by Sean Dietrich

Requests for information should be addressed to:
Zondervan, *3900 Sparks Dr. SE, Grand Rapids, Michigan 49546*

Zondervan titles may be purchased in bulk for educational, business, fundraising, or sales promotional use. For information, please email SpecialMarkets@ Zondervan.com.

Library of Congress Cataloging-in-Publication Data

Names: Dietrich, Sean, 1982- author.
Title: You are my sunshine : a story of love, promises, and a really long bike ride / Sean Dietrich.
Description: Grand Rapids, Michigan : Zondervan Books, [2022] | Series: Sean of the South
Identifiers: LCCN 2022017099 (print) | LCCN 2022017100 (ebook) | ISBN 9780310355786 (hardcover) | ISBN 9780310355830 (audio) | ISBN 9780310355793 (ebook)
Classification: LCC PS3604.I2254 Y68 2022 (print) | LCC PS3604.I2254 (ebook) | DDC 813/.6—dc23
LC record available at https://lccn.loc.gov/2022017099
LC ebook record available at https://lccn.loc.gov/2022017100

Published in association with The Bindery Agency, www.TheBinderyAgency.com.

*Cover design, illustration, and lettering: Kristi Smith, Juicebox Designs*
*Map illustration: Juicebox Designs*
*Interior design: Denise Froehlich*

*Printed in the United States of America*

22  23  24  25  26  27  28  29  30  31   /LSC/   13  12  11  10  9  8  7  6  5  4  3  2  1

I'd like to introduce the band.
To my dogs, Thelma Lou and Otis, without whom
this book would've been finished two years earlier.
To Julie, for lending me her eyes.
To Alex, without whom I would be
living in a refrigerator carton.
To Carolyn, for sticking with me, and for somehow
making me believe that I am a writer.
To my late mother-in-law, who inspired the book title.
And lastly, to my wife, who has never once
to my knowledge tried to kill me.

# Contents

## Part 3: The Chesapeake and Ohio Canal Towpath

# Our Two Heroes

*Love is friendship that has caught fire. It is
quiet understanding, mutual confidence,
sharing, and forgiving. It is loyal through good
times and bad times. It settles for less than
perfection. It allows for human weakness.*

—ANN LANDERS

A doctor found a lump in my wife's left breast and multiple masses on her ovaries. We hadn't been married long. We were young. We still looked like youthful little Kewpie dolls. Our lives had been going great. We were poor but happy. And now we were talking seriously about the *c*-word. The next thing I knew we were sitting in a medical office waiting room, where I watched a toddler play with wooden blocks and try to eat an entire *Woman's World* magazine that predated the Mesozoic era. Before long, we found ourselves seated in a tiny exam room listening to a doctor use medical-sounding words that froze my blood, words I never thought would apply to us, words like *biopsy* and *lumpectomy*. Then he threw out the words *mastectomy* and *oophorectomy*.

"But it's still too early to tell," he added. "We need to do tests."

"Tests," my wife, Jamie, and I said in unison.

He smiled weakly.

"You mean like multiple choice?" said my wife.

"Not exactly."

There was that cool, professional smile again. It looked like he'd practiced this face in the mirror a lot.

The doctor was nonchalant about what was ahead. To him this was just another day at the mill. But to us, this information was nuclear. He held the scans up to the light, pointing at them, rotating them, talking in doctor-speak. But I couldn't hear a word he said. To me, he sounded like Charlie Brown's schoolteacher. All I could think about was my vibrant wife. I was in a state of—I don't know—shock, although it also felt a little like paralysis.

I excused myself while the doctor taught my wife how to pronounce *ovarium inferum*, performing another inspection on her. Before I left the room, my wife said nothing but locked her eyes on mine. She made an unmistakable gesture that is common in my family. She held up a hand—thumb, index, and pinky extended; middle fingers down. This is sign language for "I love you."

I returned the salute.

I stood in the hall and doubled over.

I was about to puke. My mouth was dry, my chest was tight, the ambient temperature dropped. I saw myself in a mirror. My complexion had gone white, like someone had sucked the color out of my youthful world. I felt like I'd aged fifty years.

I hate going to the doctor. I hate being subjected to medical care. I hate needles, blood pressure cuffs, tongue depressors, and the medieval test where they tell a guy to turn his head and cough. But the thing I dislike most is the waiting. Everything in the world of modern medicine is based on waiting. Go call this doctor. Wait for a callback. Now call *that* doctor. Wait some more. Call *this* specialist. More waiting. Sorry, the specialist is booked solid—you'll have to wait fourteen more months. May I see your insurance provider information? Which credit card will you be using, sir? I'm gonna need your copay, policy number, Social Security number, and the blood of a nanny goat. Please sit down; the doctor will be with you shortly. And by "shortly" they mean sometime before the installation of the next pope.

The next weeks and months were a miserable time to be alive. Fear was our main emotion. We never knew anything for certain about what lay ahead, and our minds became our perpetual tormentors, always racing toward the worst-case scenario between tests.

There was a lump in my wife's breast and growths on her ovaries.

The doctor's words kept replaying in my mind, akin to an old Bob Wills record I once had that skipped whenever it got to "Cotton-Eyed Joe."

*Had not' a been for Cotton-Eyed Joe,*
*Had not' a been for Cotton-Eyed Joe,*
*Had not' a been for Cotton-Eyed Joe,*

My mother finally threw that record from a second-story window like a Frisbee, achieving incredible distance for someone who, let's be honest, threw like a girl.

The doc said it *might* be this. It *might* be that. She *might* be okay. She *might* not. After about a month, I was experiencing something that amounted to moderate psychosis. I couldn't focus. I couldn't read books, watch movies, or carry on normal conversations without thinking about that one word in the back of my brain. And the weird thing was, my wife and I became very good at not talking about the worst possibilities, even though they were present in each unspoken word or emotion that passed between us.

Finally, the fateful morning came when I drove the math teacher to the hospital for her first experience under the knife. They called it a "procedure," a frightening word. The most important human in my life was having a procedure. Lord have mercy.

I'll never forget the drive to the hospital. The mist was covering the old Florida road. Our chipped Gulf Coast highway was first commissioned in 1934, originally stretching from Apalachicola to Pensacola. At 671 miles, US Route 98 is the longest road in the Sunshine State. And yet that morning it felt about as long as my driveway.

I sat behind the wheel in a trance. The woman beside me held my hand tightly. I kept my eyes on the road and tried to remind myself to keep breathing. She needed me to be strong, that's what I kept telling myself. That's what my friends kept telling me. Be strong. Be a cheerleader. Don't jump to conclusions. Stay positive. Everything will probably be fine.

But what if things weren't fine? What if the person I loved most on this earth was being killed slowly and invisibly? I have too many family members who have died from the c-word, even more friends. Within a year, I had seen six people I love succumb to or suffer with cancer. Cancer does not discriminate. It kills children and grandparents alike.

We parked in the hospital parking lot. I shut off the car.

Why did time seem to be moving so fast? I looked at my wristwatch and thought about tossing it like my mother did with the Bob Wills record.

Soon Jamie and I were walking across a parking lot toward the towering hospital, holding hands tightly. Then came an awkward moment, just before entering the sliding doors, when we had to release hands so we wouldn't look like the kinds of fools who sit on the same side of a restaurant booth. We released. And for some reason, this letting go of hands was difficult. I can't explain why. As long as we were touching, things seemed a little better. But when we let go, this now made us two nontouching, ordinary people, adrift in the merciless world.

The thing is, I have never seen us as ordinary people. We've always been Jamie and Sean. Always in that order. Always said together. Some of my wife's high school students, however, knew me as Mister Jamie, and many of my wife's friends never even bothered to learn my name. They just called me Jamie's husband, or Whatshisface. I've always been okay with that. The most identifiable trait about me has always been her, and I wear this with pride.

My wife is loud, confrontational, type A, hyperorganized, and uses language that undermines the Southern Baptist Convention. She can hold more beer than I can and sing the national anthem louder than me. She understands the onside kick better than most jayvee quarterbacks, and she can prepare an entire squadron of pound cakes wearing a blindfold. She can captivate her second-grade Sunday school class with three words, and she is beloved by all who were fortunate enough to study math beneath her.

My wife and I tend to be animated people, and we appreciate humor. In social situations, we have our Burns-and-Allen routine down pat. We play off each other when our audience is hot and will do almost anything for a laugh. We are simple people. We get along. We disagree hard. We live in a small house. We drive old cars. We use coupons. We shop at thrift stores. We are dog lovers whose clothes are covered in dander and hair.

This woman also saved my life. Before her, I was a suicide survivor, a dropout, a construction worker, a beer-joint musician with a considerably dim future and with realy pour grammer. Jamie helped me get through college; she told me I was somebody; she tutored me in algebra, trig, liberal arts math, and the systematic, academic hell that is statistics.

We finish each other's thoughts, read each other's minds, fight each other's battles, and nobody has ever beaten us at a game of Taboo.

Taboo, for anyone who is not familiar, is a board game wherein you draw a card with a key word on it, and the object is to coax your partner to guess this word without using the hint words on the card. Our typical Taboo game goes like this:

"Okay, Jamie, this is a thing that—"

"Kangaroo."

"Right. Okay, next card. Now this is something you—"

"The Smithsonian National Museum of Natural History."

"Time's up."

Violent high five.

After we walked into the sterilized air of the hospital, a nurse took my wife's blood pressure and attempted to make small talk. Next the nurses made my wife remove her clothes and put on one of those horrible gowns. We live in the twenty-first century. We have robotic medical devices capable of performing surgery manned by a doctor 4,100 miles away. And yet patients still wear cheek-revealing gowns that predate the Dark Ages.

Jamie was soon in a wheelchair, reading a *National Geographic*, ready to be escorted to the place where biopsies happen. I sat beside her in a sticky vinyl seat, drumming my fingers on an armrest. I was sick. I ignored the TV in the corner blaring episodes of *Judge Judy* at a volume loud enough to crack porcelain. And I was trying a little too hard to be upbeat.

"It'll be fine," I said.

She drew in a breath. "Right."

"Over before you know it."

"Yes."

"They do this kind of thing every day."

"Every day. Right."

"Just a routine thing."

"Yes."

"Nothing to worry about."

I was a bad liar. What I really wanted to say was "I love you." But I'd already said it 12,203,291 times that morning, and I feared those three words had started to lose their impact.

I wanted to be the one in that wheelchair. I wanted to save the day for my wife. It should have been me going back there to be poked and sliced open.

My wife absently turned a page in her magazine. "I wanna do something fun."

I nodded.

"Something big," she said. "Something together. Something really . . . big."

"Like what?"

"Something—I dunno—big."

Judge Judy was tongue-lashing the defendant.

I was reminding myself to breathe.

She looked at me. "I'm thinking something wild. Something really, really . . ."

"Big?"

"Exactly. Something crazy."

"Like a reverse mortgage?"

My heart was not in our conversation, but I wanted to keep her talking.

"Okay, sure, sweetie," I said. "Whatever you want. We'll do something . . ."

"Big?"

"You bet."

The second hand on the clock was clicking. Judge Judy was tearing into the prosecution now. I realized I was wringing my hands.

My wife held up the magazine and tapped the page. "How about doing this?"

The glossy photo spread showed images of a trail cutting through deep woods and mountains, across rivers and creeks.

"This looks fun," she said.

I didn't answer at first because I was confused. My wife and I are not outdoorsy people. We're more Krispy Kreme enthusiasts. Even so, I smiled. "Whatever you want, honey."

"We could camp out," she said. "Sleep under the stars, and you know . . . it could be really fun."

"Sure."

"You'd do it?" she said.

I looked at the magazine closely. The pictures showed something called the C&O trail. I'd never even heard of it.

I nodded. "Why not?"

"Seriously?" she said. "You think we could do all one hundred and eighty-five miles?"

"Wait. How many miles?"

"One hundred and eighty-five."

"Um. Maybe," I said.

She smiled. "You'd really do this for me? You swear?"

"Well, let's not start swearing."

"Swear to God."

"Honey."

She plopped the magazine into her lap. "I knew it. You're just telling me what I want to hear."

"Alright. I swear to God." My Baptist mother would have disowned me.

Thus satisfied, my wife read through the magazine article while I watched her beneath the glow of the harsh lights and nearly cried.

The nurse finally came into our little room and gripped the handles of Jamie's wheelchair. She handed me the magazine. I released my wife's hand once again and felt my chin start to quiver dangerously. I followed the wheelchair down the hallway, spewing more nervous chatter. I could see the math teacher nailing a brave smile to her face. I kept pace alongside her chair until we arrived at two foreboding doors labeled "For Authorized Personnel Only."

The nurse turned to me. "Sorry, sir, this is as far as you go." The lady mashed a big button on the wall, and the doors swung open. And they took my wife away from me.

"We're going to do something big!" I called out behind them, holding up the *National Geographic*. "Something really big! This will all be over soon! You'll see!"

The doors closed.

The last thing I saw was my wife's hand, raised in an unmistakable gesture. Index, pinky, and thumb extended. Middle fingers down.

"I love you too!" I shouted to steel doors. But there was no answer.

And this is where our story begins.

# PART 1

# The Beginning

Of all the paths you
take in life, make sure a
few of them are dirt.

—JOHN MUIR

# 1

*It was the* worst of times, it was the worst of times. It was an age of wisdom, it was an age of foolishness. It was an age of mass toilet paper shortages and viral memes about cats. The pandemic was in full swing. Our lives were on lockdown. Our mailman wore a hazmat suit. And yet it was the perfect Florida Panhandle end-of-summer sunset. Birds were chattering in the branches. The sky was painted with broad brushstrokes of pink and gold. The setting sun fell upon the woods near my home like a heavy quilt of light, casting long shadows onto my driveway.

I was unemployed. The life of a writer is a gig-by-gig deal. Gigs were dead. Long live the gig. Before the pandemic, I traveled and did speaking engagements full-time and felt somewhat useful. I interviewed exceptional people. I wrote magazine articles, humorous essays, columns. I was a frequent flyer. I performed in little theaters in towns across America for audiences of snoring people. I had work. Then, poof. That fateful March, my entire calendar dried up. Jobless.

It was the summer from perdition. Jamie and I had been

married for approaching twenty years. She was a high school math teacher, and she was jobless. All we did was sit at home and look at our little mountain of bills growing on the kitchen table.

This was our worst year by far.

Also, it was quite a time to be a Floridian. Fear was in the drinking water. Almost overnight there were over 400,000 cases of COVID-19 in the Sunshine State, and the numbers were climbing like decisions at a Billy Graham crusade. That number would double in only a few months. Six people on my gravel road had the virus. Many of my friends were infected; a few died. My aunt's funeral had no attendees; the preachers wore N95 respirators. Even our mail lady contracted coronavirus and lost her job. My friend Dale celebrated his thirty-eighth birthday in the ICU. And he was lucky because the patient in bed next to him, also thirty-eight, never came home.

Hardly anyone in our neighborhood was exiting their home because COVID was still a new concept we didn't understand. It was prowling in the streets like an invisible serial killer. Nobody knew much about this disease yet, except that it was claiming several hundred people per day in New York City. Those poor New Yorkers had it rough.

I speak for most Americans when I say that my mental health had never been so bad. Every day, the news served up fresh panic on TV. The anchors kept saying that the virus had something to do with eating fruit bats, or chimpanzees, or maybe it was *El Niño*, or the stock market, or Justin Bieber—I can't remember now. Truthfully, I don't want to remember. All anyone knew was that life sucked. The world was closing for business. Theaters, hardware stores, supermarkets, bars, courthouses, schools, libraries, Dollywood.

You couldn't get away from it. That week, I had tried to get my oil changed, but the auto garage was closed because everyone in the garage had contracted the virus. Later, I would learn that the guy who normally changed my oil was fifty-nine years old and died from kidney failure. You hear stuff like this, and it plays games with your mind.

If you visited the grocery store, the cashiers wore welding masks and took your temperature with a *Star Trek*–style radar gun. You had to follow little arrows on the linoleum floor to minimize human contact and keep the flow of shoppers moving. Management recommended double masks. Suddenly going shopping felt like being in a cheap sci-fi movie wherein zombies were chasing you. Most shoppers rushed through the supermarket like they were trying to catch the last chopper out of Saigon. People were fighting about everything. Sometimes, right in the supermarket aisles.

Like I said, the worst of times.

I sat on the porch, caught in a kind of lethargic coma. The radio crackled and hissed. I spent my afternoons thinking about how I was out of a job, and how there was nothing I could do about it, and how I was just like 14 percent of America. It was the highest unemployment rate since 1948. Our meager savings account was evaporating. The only thing left to look forward to in a world of shutdowns, social distancing, mass riots, and death was baseball. And even that stunk.

Today, my ensemble was plaid PJ bottoms, a ratty T-shirt, and my palm leaf Stetson to keep the sun out of my eyes. I looked like the pride of the neighborhood. All that was missing was the Budweiser. But I'd given up drinking because too many of my friends were hitting the sauce pretty hard during the pandemic. There had been a 54 percent spike in American alcohol sales.

I had been wearing these jammies for almost four months straight without washing them. The pajama bottoms had developed a new hole in the seat of my pants. I sometimes put my finger through the new tear to amuse myself. My wife threatened to douse these raggedy pajamas in kerosene and set them on fire in the backyard, which is why I never took them off. A man has to stand his ground.

The baseball announcer's tinny voice said, "The Braves are having trouble rallying tonight, folks. Things are not looking good for the Braves . . ."

Things weren't looking particularly good for me either. Summertime felt like a depressive winter. Even sunny days seemed cloudy to me. And for some reason, I was either constantly sleepy or couldn't sleep at all. Focusing on personal writing projects was also becoming increasingly difficult. I had developed a major attention deficit disorder and found that I was having a hard time finishing anyth

Maybe I wasn't the only one who was depressed, and maybe this is part of what made the experience exponentially worse.

In the distance a small cloud of dust came hurtling up our dirt road.

It was a minivan with a single flashing orange light. The mail guy. My dogs started going crazy. I told them to sit, a command they dutifully ignored. The vehicle skidded to a stop beside our mangled mailbox, hazards blinking. Our poor mail receptacle had become the recent victim of the annual sophomore mailbox baseball playoffs. And from the size of the dent, I'd say it had been an outfield double.

The mail guy wore two surgical masks, yellow rubber dishwashing gloves, and what looked like a lead X-ray vest from the dentist's office. He carefully shoved mail into our twisted box and then sanitized his hands. He was new to our rural mail route and had been making mistakes all over the place, driving his minivan in perpetual confusion, cramming mail into wrong mailboxes so that everyone in my neighborhood was either delinquent on important bills or about to get evicted.

I waved at him. He did not wave back.

When he drove away, I shuffled across the sandy road toward our cockeyed receptacle, lid dangling open, flag bent at ninety degrees. Immediately I realized the mail guy had delivered the wrong mail. Again. Third time in a row. It was only a matter of time before the power company shut off my lights and the IRS confiscated my liver.

I rifled through the stack of letters. Not a single envelope belonged to me. They were all bills for someone named Albert, who doesn't even live on my street. I don't know anyone named Albert. I don't think anyone is named Albert. Albert's mail was the usual stuff: real estate flyers, a clothing catalog, a pamphlet about mail-order meat products from Nebraska, two credit card offers, and one plastic-wrapped magazine.

The magazine looked interesting. So I opened the plastic with my thumbnail and hoped Albert wouldn't mind; these were desperate times.

It was a fitness magazine. On the front were two very trim people who looked like Swedish underwear models, completely devoid of body hair and adipose tissue. They were shirtless, covered in strategically positioned Lycra skivvies, both with rippling muscles and skimpy attire that left nothing to my fundamentalist imagination. I flipped through the pages and smirked at the impossible bodies, concrete thighs, and airbrushed buns of bronze. I stopped flipping when I reached an article titled "America's Woods."

The cover photo showed stunning photographs of a nature trail mostly located on the Eastern Seaboard. "Visit Maryland and Bike the C&O Trail," the article title read. It was ringing a faint bell in my brain. I tried to recall where I'd heard about this particular trail before, but it wasn't coming to me.

I stopped flipping pages when I sensed a nosy certified math teacher looking over my shoulder at the magazine. I could feel her breath on my neck.

She yanked the magazine from my hands and said, "It's a sign."

The worst of times, I tell you.

You could watch the whole American shipwreck unfolding on your TV screen. The world had gone slap nuts. I was glued to the televised disaster playing out in New York. After a wave of springtime infections, patients were outnumbering hospital beds. Field hospital tents were erected in Central Park. Medical workers in yellow jumpsuits were storing the deceased in freezer trucks parked on side streets in Brooklyn. The US Army, the National Guard, and the Air National Guard were removing bodies from homes. Restaurants in the West Village were plywooding windows. Chinatown was dead, maybe forever. Someone put a face mask on Prometheus outside Rockefeller Center. And it was on the tube twenty-four seven.

It's no wonder the United States Census Bureau found that *one-third* of Americans were likely clinically depressed. One-third. This means that roughly the total population of seventeen US states was experiencing psychic trauma. Suicide rates were higher than they'd been since World War II. The world couldn't have been more upside down. Political demonstrators were storming town squares. Rioters were setting cars on fire and flogging each other with objects that weren't pool noodles.

And while I realize this is all very depressing to read about, I bring this up for an important reason because at the same time, something unusual was happening in North America. Americans were rediscovering the outdoors like crazy.

There were unparalleled numbers of visitors to public lands. In 2020, there were record-breaking reports of thru-hikers on the Appalachian Trail. And even though the trail had been, technically, closed for the pandemic, the thru-hikes outnumbered those from previous years. Fifteen national parks set new visitation records. Five broke attendance records. You could not keep people out of the woods. Least of all the woman I married.

I had never seen my wife so hell-bent on doing something, except for the time she was convinced I needed to start eating raisins to boost my iron levels. I hate raisins.

"This is *it*," she said, slapping the magazine. "This is our sign."

"Would you listen to yourself? It's not a sign. It's just a magazine."

"This is our *something big*."

"You've lost your mind."

"Don't you remember?" she said. "We said we were gonna do *something big*."

I shook my head and refilled my coffee. "Honolulu is big."

"I've been asking for a sign."

"An inground pool is big."

It seemed like a hundred years since her first biopsy. The results had showed that her tumors were benign. But anyone who has been through a cancer scare knows that it's not over when it's over. Throughout the years we'd gone through more checkups, more biopsies, more exams, more medical hell, more insomnia. And each time Jamie went in for screenings we found ourselves holding our collective breath until our faces looked like black cherries.

Thankfully, everything was okay. But we had never even discussed the *something big* we'd said we were going to do in the hospital waiting room years earlier, probably because you say things sometimes when you're under the gun. And nobody expects you to actually follow through on those promises.

My wife tossed the magazine onto the kitchen table. "I think we should do it."

"Do what? Can you hear yourself?"

"Don't you remember the promise *you made me?*"

"That was a long time ago and—"

"You told me we would do this."

"I was just trying to—"

"Then you swore to God."

Silence.

The magazine's two-page spread showed nothing but trees. A mountain trail cut through undulating clusters of big, towering, prehistoric-looking conifers. Another photo showed a man riding a bicycle in an obscenely green forest, camping gear mounted on the back of his bike. His teeth were unnaturally white. He was dwarfed by the enormity of red maples and American beeches behind him, like a gnat. The caption read: "The Great Allegheny Passage trail, and the Chesapeake and Ohio Canal towpath."

"I don't believe in coincidences," she said. "This is a sign."

"Sweetie, we're in the middle of a global lockdown."

"I'll never forget when you promised me . . ."

"Sweetie."

". . . Then you promised the Lord."

She must have read the article aloud fifty times. She talked about the trails from breakfast until she clicked off her nightstand lamp. These trails cast a strange magic over her. I suppose there are some things in this life that cannot be explained. Like the color of water. Or the exact shade of a sunset. Black Friday madness is another inexplicable thing: Why don't people buy their flat screens on Wednesday? Not everything can be articulated in this life. Least of all the inner workings of the complex mind of Jamie Martin Dietrich.

Over the next days, our lives took on a new sense of purpose. I played along at first, but if I'm being honest, this whole idea struck me as nonsensical. It was so foolish, in fact, I was sure it would blow over. After all, we had several things going against us. For starters, middle age. Secondly, we're not bikers. You fall off a bike when you're young, and you laugh with your pals and go grab an ice-cold malted beverage. You fall off a bike on the wrong side of forty, and the doctor hands your spouse a do-not-resuscitate order form. I despise bikes. The last time I rode a bike I bruised three ribs and nearly fractured my wrist. The only thing I dislike more than bikes would be, perhaps, nuclear war.

Also, I am not much of an outdoorsman anymore. I used to love to camp, and I still love fishing, but something happens when you grow up. You slowly become divorced from nature. Your idea of camping is to buy a twenty-eight-foot RV and fall gracefully into the loving embrace of central air-conditioning. As a boy I once lived for the thrill of being lost among trees. As a teenager I tent camped all the time—although it was always within arm's reach of a vending machine. But the romance of the outdoors had faded for me over the years. And besides, this trail was different. This was a remote woodland path in the heart of the mid-Atlantic. This was miles and miles from civilization. This wasn't a trail. This was the book of Exodus.

"It's a sign," she said.

"This is insane," I said.

Then came the fateful morning when the math teacher went too far. I awoke to find her fully dressed in what appeared to be professional jogging clothes, wearing a bright green John Deere cap. She was standing over my sleeping body, holding a bowl of cold Quaker Oats.

"Get changed," she said. "We start training today."

I wiped the crusted sleep from my eyes. "Why are you eating oatmeal?"

"This isn't my oatmeal. It's yours."

"But I hate oatmeal."

"It's okay. I put raisins in it."

My wife forced me into workout clothes, and I found myself donning a pair of dated nylon shorts. And we went for a vigorous walk through the morning sunlight. We walked for three miles, until my hamstrings tightened and my heels became blistered and I was begging to go back. Which, of course, was impossible. We would never be going back to the way things were before.

Mysteriously, my pajamas were never seen again.

# 2

*On the morning* of May 21, 1975, a little yellow train left the Baltimore & Ohio Railroad depot in Pittsburgh for the last time. The diesel engine plunged through the Allegheny Forest of Pennsylvania like a bygone bullet, the way it had done twenty-two million times before. It was a Chessie System locomotive. Behind it was an Amtrak Silver Dome locomotive, followed by an old Western Maryland coach. The three trains were bound for Cumberland, Maryland. After this farewell tour of Appalachia, the railroad would be disbanded and abandoned. It would be replaced with a bike trail, of all things.

Spectators and train enthusiasts lined the tracks to say goodbye to an American era. Children waved to engineers as they passed. Passengers leaned out the locomotive windows and waved to their admirers. Grandparents on the sidelines told train stories to toddlers on their hips. At one time, all American grandparents had train stories.

In the backwater of Rockwood, Pennsylvania (pop. 890), an elderly man named Maynard Stembower was watching the engines go by with moistened eyes. Maynard had once rooted himself in this exact spot in 1912 to watch the first train cross these mid-Atlantic tracks. Now he was a witness to the train's funeral march. Soon these tracks would be paved with tarmac and swarming with young people who pedaled Schwinns and Huffys.

Converting 150 miles of railroad into one of the longest paved nature trails in the United States was no small feat. But trail devotees were optimistic. One *New York Times* reporter asked a local man how long he thought this new trail conversion might take to complete. The excited response was, "A year or two."

The guy who said this was off by a few decades. It took thirty-five years to complete the GAP trail.

The GAP finally opened in its entirety in 2013. Today, the rail-trail is considered one of the best rail-trails in the country, spanning five counties in southwestern Pennsylvania and western Maryland. The trail draws about one million visitors each year from around the globe. In fact, during typical years, there is a great international presence on the trail, and you will occasionally find yourself speaking to fellow trail goers in fluent hand gestures.

If you ride from north to south, you begin in Pittsburgh and are carried through the immense Allegheny section of the Appalachians, skirting along three rivers, through the Cumberland Narrows, across the Laurel Highlands, over the Eastern Continental Divide, and over the Mason-Dixon Line.

There, the trail finally spits you onto *another* trail. The

Chesapeake and Ohio Canal towpath. That's where the real fun begins. Because the C&O is an entirely different, more adrenal experience. The C&O is where bicycles go to die. "The grand old ditch," they call it. And that's exactly what it is. A big, beautiful, swampy, festering ditch. The C&O Canal towpath has been in use since the 1780s, which was probably the last time anyone took a Weed Eater to it.

These are long, *long* trails. Longer than anything I've ever walked. I've hiked public trails before, sure, but never anything more than a few miles. And I was never out of eyeshot from a water fountain. The GAP and C&O trails, however, lead you across Pennsylvania, Maryland, West Virginia, Virginia, through Georgetown, and eventually end in Washington, DC. Together the two trails form a distance that is roughly equivalent to the length of Kansas.

Kansas, for crying out loud.

This was more than *something big*. This was a 350-mile wilderness campaign. This was the kind of thing you trained for, otherwise you ended up with a pulled groin in the middle of the Virginia wilderness playing patty cake with coyotes.

Moreover, pedaling across four US states isn't exactly what guys like me would call fun. In my mind, the term *having fun* involves, at minimum, a twenty-four-hour pizza buffet. But there was no talking my wife out of it. Every time I tried to speak to her, she got this faraway look in her eyes. And I could see that she was already out there, somewhere on the trail.

My wife is a voracious researcher. She spent her days

reading about the trails, obsessing over the trails, pouring over magazines and websites. She is a woman who, solely using Google and YouTube, could figure out how to run a neurosurgery department. She was waking up early in the mornings to study the GAP trail and everything related to it. She also read up on bicycles, camping gear, backpacks, the most effective kinds of torniquets, and bear spray.

You probably think I'm exaggerating, but that's only because you don't know my wife. I'd often find her at the computer, hunched over the keyboard, price comparing, reading articles aloud, or watching shaky footage filmed by people who had already done the trails with cameras mounted on their helmets. This genie was not going back in the bottle.

One of the first things you are confronted with when you consider hiking a great distance is that completing any trail in a modern society is essentially a purposeless endeavor. Think about it. Give me one logical reason for doing a 350-mile trail. Go ahead, I'll wait.

See? You can't do it. Trust me, I've tried. I still can't come up with a good reason for doing a trail, let alone a reason for writing an entire book about one. The pioneer days are over; we aren't exploring for land, gold, or access to clean water anymore. We have SUVs, interstates, and Burger Kings now. Why would anyone willingly live like a homeless person for days on end and survive on MRE rations? Why would a normal person risk the dangers associated with the wilderness? And yes, there are plenty of life-threatening dangers out there.

One morning I found my wife staring at a laptop monitor with bloodshot eyes and messed-up hair. On her screen was a picture of a dead man, lying in the prone position. The headline read: "Know the Dangers of Dehydration."

"We're gonna need electrolyte packets," said Jamie, making a note on her legal pad.

Only a year before we would do the trail, a thirty-two-year-old woman in superb physical shape had died from heat exhaustion on the C&O towpath. She was found unconscious, lying near the Potomac. This was a woman who was a veteran hiker who knew her way along these trails. This was someone who hiked every weekend and was familiar with electrolyte packets. This was a woman in her *thirties*.

There were more war stories like this. Many more. And the math teacher read them all with a sort of twisted morbid delight. I won't say Jamie became fixated on death, but she was quickly becoming one of America's leading experts on trail fatalities. Each morning while I poured coffee, my wife would deliver agonizing accounts of trail disasters, describing the various ways trail enthusiasts could die.

A man in his sixties lost control of his cycle on the C&O Canal towpath, flew over his handlebars, fell into a canal lock, and died instantly. A fifty-six-year-old guy died on the C&O while biking with a friend through a rainstorm when—get this—a tree fell on him. Trees fall all the time out there. Many bikers report watching trees with bases as big as Buicks falling right beside them. Imagine hearing the deep, groaning sound of a tree just before watching it slam into the earth and turn your innards into tapioca. Or better yet, let's say the tree doesn't kill you per se, but only pins you down. Then along come Yogi and Boo Boo.

People had been murdered in these remote regions. Attacked. Raped. Stabbed. Unidentified bodies are sometimes retrieved from the C&O canal. These are uninhabited historic lands. Anything could happen out there.

Not long before we would take the trail, an attacker was at large on the GAP, dubbed by newspersons as "the bike trail attacker." News reports said the attacker was in his twenties or thirties, possibly nonverbal. He had appeared out of the woods wearing no shirt, jeans rolled up to his ankles, and he tried to rape a woman who was riding on the GAP. The police had been unsuccessfully looking for the attacker, combing the woods with dogs and flying drones. He was still on the loose.

The high school teacher also had a taste for the exotic, so she kept me abreast of developments regarding Bigfoot. I learned that Pennsylvania has a record of 1,304 sightings of Bigfoot. The state ranks in the top three for Bigfoot appearances. They celebrate Bigfoot Day in Clearfield, for heaven's sake. Suffice it to say, if you're looking for Sasquatch, the Allegheny National Forest is where you go.

But the most thrilling parts of my wife's investigation, by far, were the internet searches that turned up home movies featuring well-known predators with a taste for human organ meat. My wife would lie in bed holding her phone for the two of us to watch homespun video montages of mountain lions climbing trees, swinging from limbs, clawing open nylon backpacks, and just generally scaring the dookie out of anyone nearby.

Both trails are riddled with cougars, many of which have been captured by university researchers, tagged, then released back into the wild. I could just imagine trotting into the woods to use the restroom one morning and happening upon a cougar with a blinking GPS collar bearing the logo for Penn State.

Also, rodents. Big, fat, violent woodland rats, with family members doing time in San Quentin. Rats carry hantavirus pulmonary syndrome. In 2012, a hantavirus outbreak infected overnight visitors at Yosemite National Park, causing officials to demolish ninety-one tent camping areas. That same year, a man hiking the Adirondacks contracted HPS in New York. So we were looking at a nationwide trend.

Spiders are also bad on the trail. I don't like spiders. Every spider I have ever seen is either a black widow or a Brazilian wandering spider capable of bringing down a herd of water buffalo.

Also, I'm deathly allergic to poison ivy. I get poison ivy so badly that I require steroids to prevent my airways from closing. The C&O towpath is the world's most pristine poison ivy patch. I was actually glad to learn about the poison ivy problems because this was my trump card. Now I had an out.

When my wife was reading a trail guidebook in bed one night, I let her have it.

"What a shame we can't go," I said.

"What're you talking about?"

"The poison ivy."

"What about it?"

"I can't be around poison ivy. You know that stuff could kill me. What a bummer. I'm really sorry."

I gave a frowny face.

She shook her head, licked a thumb, then turned a page. "Nope. Poison ivy won't be your biggest problem out there. *Your* biggest problem will be all the snakes."

There was no way in twelve hells I was doing this trail.

# 3

Hanna Eskland was four years old, hiking with her father and brother on the C&O towpath, when she shouted, "It pinched me, it pinched me!" They were a long way from civilization. At first, Hanna's father thought a bee or maybe a wasp had stung her on the foot. But they were not so lucky. When he glanced at the dirt path, he saw something quickly slithering toward them, not away from them.

"Ssssssssssssss!" said the creature.

Amazingly, a passerby came along at just the right moment. Hanna's father borrowed the person's bike and—demonstrating the power of adrenaline—carried a four-year-old to the ranger station in Great Falls Tavern on a bike, *in his lap.* By then, Hanna's foot was discolored. The park rangers took Hanna in, called an ambulance, and tried to keep her comfortable. But the rangers turned out to be unequipped for snakebites.

It bears remembering that this event occurred in a national historical park that is maintained by the US government, part of a system funded by an annual three billion in federal tax dollars and manned by a company of uniformed law enforcement officers who have been charged with the responsibility of overseeing 184.5 miles of trails. And yet, apparently, it had never occurred to the officials that someone might get bitten by a snake out there.

When Hanna got to the ranger station, all they could do was elevate her foot.

After a copperhead strikes, you don't have time for hemming and hawing. Edema occurs withing minutes, and the swelling soon becomes cartoonish. People's ankles turn into watermelons. You have maybe four hours to administer antivenom; otherwise you're gambling. If you wait much longer than eight hours, you might as well hire a qualified preacher. The stopwatch for Hanna had just started.

The ambulance arrived. They raced Hanna to Suburban Hospital in Bethesda, a twenty-minute ride. At the ER, the medical staff told Hanna's father they didn't stock antivenom. So they life-flighted Hanna to Children's National Medical Center in Washington, DC, where—surprise—they, too, did not stock antivenom. After what seemed like a bad stage farce, the antivenin treatment had to be flown in from Manassas, Virginia, where it was finally administered to Hanna, whose foot was big enough to have its own talk show. The treatment worked. Thank God.

But all this leads the crack investigative journalist in me to ask the important question: "Would this have happened at a Sandals all-inclusive Jamaican resort?"

I do not like snakes. I have been avoiding them my entire

life. My first traumatic encounter with a snake was in the first grade when a local zoo worker brought a fourteen-foot boa constrictor into our classroom. I screamed so loud I blacked out. After passing out, I remember opening my eyes to discover I was being escorted to the nurse's office to borrow a loaner pair of trousers.

I had another traumatic experience with snakes when I was playing in the woods with my friend Martin Wannamaker, directly behind my childhood home. Martin fell into a puddle and several snakes covered his arms and legs. The creatures turned out to be moccasins. They rushed Martin to the doctor and administered treatment. There was not a mother within five counties who didn't know the chilling tale of Martin Wannamaker and who wasn't constantly reminding us to "watch out for snakes" during our Sunday school prayers.

So this was the end of all arguments. There was no getting around the snakes. Even my wife realized the error she'd made by bringing up the topic. She attempted to backpedal, but the damage had been done. No amount of pointing out the positives of the trail could convince me to pitch a tent in Snakeville, USA. Although she definitely tried. At one point my wife even called a park ranger on the phone and had a conversation about snakes for my benefit. The park ranger was extremely helpful and said snakes were nothing to worry about on the trails. I couldn't help but notice, however, that this particular "park ranger" sounded suspiciously like my mother-in-law.

I gave my wife a firm no, once and for all. We were not going on the trail. It was not feasible. It was not wise. It wasn't plausible. It didn't matter what kind of promises we made to each other two decades ago. This was real life. We were not youngsters. My answer was final. This expedition could not happen. It would not happen. No way, no how.

"It's really going to happen!" said my wife.

My wife had just hung up the phone and successfully booked our shuttle from Washington, DC, to Pittsburgh. She had written details on our refrigerator calendar, and she had already *bought a fanny pack*. This was not a drill.

She was cheerfully chopping vegetables on a cutting board, talking incessantly about the innumerable differences between inflatable sleeping mats and foam mats. And I felt as though I were losing ground.

"Now hold on," I said. "I can't believe you'd force me into this. I haven't agreed to anything yet."

She was talking more to herself than me. "We're gonna need to start shopping for supplies, I need to make an inventory checklist, gotta call a pet sitter . . ."

"Jamie."

". . . gonna need hiking shoes, all-weather jackets, flashlights . . ."

"Are you listening to me? Snakes. There are snakes."

". . . first aid kits, calamine lotion, life insurance policies . . ."

"And poison ivy. Do you realize what would happen if I got poison ivy out there? I could die from an allergic reaction."

She didn't even hear me.

"Do you want me to die?"

She stopped cutting. "My mother said we can borrow some of her steroids."

My wife doesn't do anything halfheartedly. Once she announces that she's doing something, it's already three-quarters done. This is a woman who once spent six months preparing the aperitif menu for her three-year-old niece's Disney-themed birthday party.

Over the following weeks, our home became filled with stacks of books about the trails, outdoor catalogs, trail maps, wilderness guides, and information packets. Her devotion to the trail was unwavering. Every afternoon a UPS truck would deliver some new piece of high-tech survival finery I never knew existed. Things like waterproof toilet paper holders, solar phone chargers, commercial-grade salmon jerky, and poop shovels. Our family room steadily expanded beneath mounds of saddlebags, dry bags, sleeping bags, wet bags, garment bags, plastic bags, laundry bags, toiletry bags, and every other specialized bag imaginable. And my wife had purchased about seventeen thousand grass-fed beef sticks.

I inspected one such meat stick by peeling back the wrapper and probing it. It had the same texture as Baltic granite.

"What is this?" I said.

"It's high-quality protein."

I took a bite. It tasted like a creosote railroad tie. "Why'd you buy so many?"

"Clearance."

The magic word.

Amazingly, beef sticks notwithstanding, we still had no bikes. You couldn't find bikes for sale within a five-hundred-mile radius. The pandemic caused worldwide bike shortages among bike manufacturers. This lack of bikes, however, did not dissuade the algebra whiz. She would find bikes. I had no doubt.

At bedtime I would often discover my wife gnawing on compressed protein sticks and using her smartphone to research bikes, or to review camping gear she'd recently purchased online. Other times, I would find that my old pillow had disappeared, only to be replaced with a special memory-foam camping pillow about the size of a *Reader's Digest*. Once, I awoke to find my wife draped in a lightweight tinfoil thermal survival blanket capable of withstanding subzero blizzards. Whenever she moved, she crinkled like a bag of Fritos.

So we were all in; this was happening. We'd already obtained a waterproof toilet paper holder.

Our refrigerator was covered in magazine clippings of the trails. The trail manuals in our bathroom had bookmarks tucked between the pages. One night I took out our trash and discovered a new bumper sticker on my wife's SUV that read:

TRAIL LIFE: IF YOU DIE, WE SPLIT YOUR GEAR

My wife's giddiness, however, reached its apex when our tent arrived in the mail. The woman was like a child who'd gotten an Easy Bake Oven for Christmas. She thanked the

UPS guy so profusely that he edged away from our doorstep and broke into a sprint. I was afraid my wife was about to chase him and try to give him beef sticks.

Our den was a glorified display for Bass Pro Shops, and her tableau now had its penultimate centerpiece. A bright yellow dome tent. My wife stood back and admired her masterstroke, her arm slung around my shoulder. It was a three-season tent ($239.00), three feet high, with state-of-the-art fabric. Once the tent was erected, she turned off the lights, donned her coal miner's headlamp ($42.95), and crawled through the zipper flap.

"Are you coming in?" she called.

I let out a big breath and looked skyward. I was wondering what kinds of legal loopholes one had to jump through to get a loved one committed.

"I'm coming."

"Bring me another protein stick."

I lowered my six-foot-one frame into the Barbie tent, nestled into my sleeping bag ($98.99), positioned myself atop a foam sleeping pad ($39.99), and marveled at how this was rapidly becoming the most expensive night's sleep we would ever have ($1,292,450.99).

My wife took my hand in her own, and I could feel her energy. We had been married for a while, and yet I'd never seen this side of her. We lay in stillness, and I could practically feel her smiling.

"Isn't this cool?" she said.

I looked at her. "Define cool."

If I'm being honest, she was right. It was novel. Maybe I was finally starting to buy into the whole idea. Or perhaps, and we cannot rule this out, I was starting to exhibit early signs of a nervous breakdown.

"You know," she said, "I wasn't sure what to expect, sleeping in a tent, but this is fun."

"This is your first time in a tent?"

"No. I camped once at the Alabama June Jam festival."

"Which year?"

"When Billy Ray Cyrus was there."

"'The achy breaky big mistakey."

"Yeah, but it wasn't real camping." She scooted closer to me. Her toes were like dry ice. "I guess I always thought camping would be a lot worse."

"Honey. This is our living room. It will be worse."

She was unfazed. "But we're actually doing this, aren't we?"

"You realize this is ridiculous, don't you?" I said. "We're out of our minds. We're not even outdoorsy people."

"You only live once."

"Yeah, but only if you do it right."

She squeezed my hand. I realized that the "one-third of depressed persons" included more persons than just me.

"I want this," she said.

"I know you do."

Tears were shed. She had been saving them up for a while. As I said, it had been a long year.

We wrapped our arms around each other, and she tucked her head into my shoulder. It makes me feel strong to hold her like that. Don't misunderstand me: I am not a strong man; I'm an incredibly weak one. But I like it when this woman pretends that I am more. I hope God is gracious enough to let us pretend for many more years.

"Hey," the mathematician said, just before sleep fell upon us. "Wanna know something?"

"What?"

"*Sssssssssssssss!*"

# PART 2

# The Great Alleghery Passage

Look deep into nature, and
then you will understand
everything better.

—ALBERT EINSTEIN

## 4

*During boyhood, being* in the woods was natural for me. When did I change? When did I become so indoorsy? I grew up as a rural child, living life among the sticks and the stubbled alfalfa fields. The entirety of my childhood happened in the forest. I knew every hemlock, birch, elm, and magnolia. I knew where to catch frogs, where the creek bed turned into red clay, where wild strawberries grew, how to catch catfish with a trotline, and how to build lean-to forts that, with enough imagination, resembled the Alamo. I knew every abandoned Studebaker and rusted Packard, and where old man Randall Watts hid booze so his wife wouldn't find it. I knew how to avoid the snakes, I knew how to watch out for poison ivy, and I knew how to leap from a rope swing into the treacherously shallow water of Camp Creek. These things didn't frighten me back then. In fact, I was rarely frightened as a boy. When did the new me take over?

I know when. On the fateful afternoon of my father's end, I had just emerged from the woods. I was covered in cockleburs and mud, reeking of little-kid sweat, when I saw the preacher's red truck pulling into our driveway. It was a rusty truck. In our world, men called to ministry were not allowed to own nice things.

I saw the truck idling upon the gravel, and I knew something was wrong.

The motor died. The preacher stepped out of his vehicle. He was wearing a necktie. I felt my circulation stop. Preachers only wear neckties to your house for two reasons. One of those reasons is Sunday dinner. This was a Wednesday evening.

When I got closer, I found that the preacher's eyes had pink rings around them. And his cheeks were wet.

The preacher told me my father was dead. And I will never forget the primal reflex that shot through my eleven-year-old body. It was fear. I needed to run. I needed to move my legs. I bolted back into the woods from whence I came. I found a rock where my father and I used to sit and look at the Milky Way in the evenings. I sat there until night fell. I wept for nearly four hours and nobody bothered me. They all knew where I was. I was in the woods.

The evening before my father died, his mind snapped and he had made a serious attempt to kill my family. On his last night alive, he pointed a .357 revolver wrapped in an old T-shirt at us and used threatening words. I don't know why he used the T-shirt. The quiet man he normally was disappeared in a flash of violence. He had lost his sanity and waved a muzzle at my mother and me, finger on the trigger, spittle forming at the corners of his mouth. My mother was battered and bleeding. My little sister was trembling. Everyone was crying and screaming. It was the longest evening of my life. And the darkest.

Three hours later my father was apprehended by Leavenworth County deputies bearing riot guns. They came crashing through our windows and shouting things like, "Hands where I can see them!" and "Get on the ground!"

I watched my father hit the ground like Raggedy Andy beneath the weight of county muscle. The last time I ever saw him alive he was crawling into the backseat of a patrol car with his hands in steel cuffs. The next day my father's brother posted bail. Hours later, they found my father dead in his brother's garage in Parkville, Missouri. Cause of death: rifle wound. Self-inflicted. They had to use dental records to identify his remains.

I realize this chapter doesn't carry the same lighthearted tone as the rest of the book, but this is the period of my life when New Me took over. After my father's death, I was always afraid. I lived beneath the heavy cloak of fear. Fear of everything.

I lost the ability to smile. To laugh. To cut loose and have fun. I was unable to fantasize. To focus. To sleep. I freely admit that I was wholly and thoroughly screwed up. In many ways, I still am. In today's world, doctors would say that little boy had clinical depressive disorder, brought on by posttraumatic stress syndrome. But back then my people called it, "Aw, hell, the boy's fine."

The fear got so bad I started having panic attacks. Sometimes I couldn't breathe at night. Other times I went three or four days without sleeping. Then I developed a bleeding ulcer, an issue that could only be corrected by something called "suppositories." These were administered by Mama after supper. Trust me, no matter how bad your life gets, it becomes a little worse when suppositories enter the picture.

I quit my baseball team. I quit talking to friends. My family quit going to church for a few years. My mother quit her job. My baby sister quit kindergarten and wouldn't learn to read until she was approaching her midtwenties. I quit school, skipped high school, and made an absolute wreck of my academic life. I became a dropout.

So I guess that's when it happened. I guess that's when I lost my connection with the marvelous outdoors. I let fear start calling the shots.

Life went on. I grew into a redheaded adolescent with exactly seventy-nine freckles on his face and nose. I was unattractive and quiet. I was withdrawn. My mother started cutting my hair to save money, so I often looked like an unusually young Navy SEAL. I was trapped in a chubby, Danny Partridge body, and I couldn't get out. And I would have probably stayed pitiful forever . . .

But then I met someone.

My life changed when I met a young brunette who had just finished culinary school and was working in a hospital kitchen. After our initial meeting, something just clicked. I visited the hospital every afternoon just to eat fried catfish and be near her. She was animated, unique, loud, and opinionated. She made me laugh. She had two college degrees and was dabbling with the idea of getting a third degree in math. I'd never met anyone like her. Why would anyone have three degrees and not work for the CIA?

Everything about this girl was intense, spunky, and in your face. To her, life was to be frontally assaulted. She did not retreat from the things the world threw at her; she kickboxed her way through them. This was a woman who frequently went into the auto mechanic's garage and stood over the mechanic's shoulder with a notepad, demanding that he explain exactly what he was doing to her air filter and why. Several local garages no longer take her business.

I married Jamie one December day in a tiny church, and my life never went back to being pathetic. I married her not only because I fell in love with her but also because she was good medicine. Her tonic helped me become the me I always wanted to be. She was patient with me. She was my one-woman cheering section. The woman made me feel as though I wasn't a stupid, frightened, lost hick, but a man with some-thing to say. I had purpose when I was with her.

Over time, with her help, I went from being a construction-working bar musician to being a graduate from a tiny community college who proudly and painstakingly maintained a 1.9 GPA. Soon thereafter, at the math teacher's urging, I became a professional writer—which still surprises me. And if you've read this far, this undoubtedly surprises you too.

The first magazine article I ever had published was sent

in without my knowing by an anonymous woman whom the magazine identified by the pseudonym *Sean's Wife*.

And so it was, one summer night, my twenty-year-old truck plunged across the southeastern United States like a rust-colored streak, bound for the mid-Atlantic. We bolted along I-85 through the beating heart of North Carolina at four in the morning. My back was sore. My joints were stiff from being behind the wheel for so long. We were bound for the Allegheny Mountains to do something that was indeed *big*. And probably idiotic.

I am a middle-aged man with a soft middle who cuts his grass with a drink holder mounted to his lawnmower handle. I had no business braving the wild. But here we were.

The long, sloping fields of the Old North State zipped by my windows in perfect blackness. Our backseat was filled with expensive camping gear and outdoor-resistant luggage that I would never use again. The back of my truck contained two used cycles. A two-wheeled bike for Jamie and one strange-looking adult tricycle she bought on craigslist for her gangly, uncoordinated life partner.

My wife slept in the passenger seat beside me, head resting against the window, snoring, with a thin line of drool hanging from her mouth. We had been on the road for four days, sleeping in inexpensive motels and eating subpar continental breakfasts. But we were doing it. We were really doing it.

Outside my windshield, the Carolina sun was about to rise. The sky was turning a grayish pink. This magnificent

Appalachian sunup only hinted at the upcoming trials that awaited two very middle-aged, very out-of-shape people who were naive enough to ride a lonesome trail.

I pushed the brim of my father's old Stetson upward on my head and took it all in. One of my hands rested on the steering column; my other reached across the bench seat to touch the hand of the woman beside me.

We passed the large welcome-to-our-state sign that read, "Virginia Is for Lovers."

I looked at the woman beside me.

"It certainly is," I said.

## 5

*Our shuttle driver* threw the gearshift of the minivan into park.

"We're here," he said. "Welcome to Pittsburgh, backbone of America. Now everybody get outta my van."

His name was Bob. He was a local. Bob was a portly, talkative guy, covered in white whiskers, with a staccato Eastern accent and a deep affection for unfiltered Camels. He'd driven four hours south from the 'Burgh to Washington, DC, to pick us up and drove another four hours north to Pittsburgh's trailhead at Point State Park downtown.

It was a cold September morning in America's Spinal Column, and we were running dangerously low on sleep. Not the way you want to start a four-state bike trip. We crawled out of the tobacco-fogged Chrysler Town & Country to find ourselves standing beneath the towering skyscrapers and smokestacks of an old steel town. We couldn't have been more disoriented if we'd woken up with our heads sewn to the carpet. My truck was parked three states away in Virginia in a public parking area. We were 1,014.19 miles from our

Florida home. To say we felt naked only hints at what we were experiencing.

"Welcome to paradise," said Bob, gesturing at the maddening cityscape. "The nation's Pitt'."

An emergency vehicle shot by us with sirens blaring and blue lights flashing. Then came two more. Also nearby we saw a homeless man vomiting into a storm sewer.

"Be it ever so humble," said Bob.

We looked at Point State Park. It is not a park, at least not like we'd expected. You hear the word *park*, and you envision greenery, maybe a few elms, picnic tables, and kids playing Frisbee. That's not what we saw before us. Point State Park is a tribute to the Age of Concrete, with all the subtle charm of a Soviet bunker.

And bridges. Pittsburgh loves its bridges. There were suspension bridges, arch bridges, beam bridges, and through-truss bridges everywhere. Bob told us that Pittsburgh has 446 bridges—that's more than Venice, Rome, or any other city in the world. Bob had been doling out tidbits like this all morning. He happily shared every hometown fact he'd ever learned since third grade.

"Pittsburgh has more annual days of rain and snow than Seattle." "Lewis and Clark started their journey right here in Pittsburgh." "Pittsburgh held the first World Series." "Pittsburgh has more Catholic relics than anywhere else in the world except the Vatican."

"Huh," we kept answering, silently praying that he'd run out of Camels.

But now we were deposited on a cold sidewalk with nothing but our cycles and our tonnage of gear scattered around us.

"Nice hat," Bob said to me. "Never seen anyone ride a bike in a cowboy hat. Looks kinda dumb, you ask me."

We were off to a great start.

"He's not riding a bike," said the math teacher. "It's a *trike*."

Bob scratched his thinning hair. "But why?"

"Because he's afraid of bikes," said Jamie.

I smiled.

Bob stared at my odd-shaped tricycle. "You're afraid of bikes?"

"Also clowns," added my wife.

Bob touched my side mirror. "Ain't never seen a bike with three wheels before. It's so . . . low to the ground."

"It's *very* safe," said the math teacher.

Bob seemed concerned.

I ignored them and kept loading my saddlebags. Although I must admit, my recumbent trike was a little silly looking beneath the soaring cityscape of Pittsburgh. The thing looked faintly reminiscent of a motorcycle sidecar, minus the dignity. The math teacher bought the trike used for a few hundred bucks, which solved the problem of my bicycle phobia, but it brought me new problems. Namely, it looked like I was riding a Barcalounger.

Bob tilted his head. "You don't actually plan on taking that thing on the C&O trail, do you?"

"I do. Why do you ask?"

"You'll never make it on that thing."

"What?"

"There's a lotta rough trail out there. I don't think your toy is up to it."

My wife and I exchanged looks.

"I'm sure he'll be fine," said my wife.

Bob handed me a business card. "You just keep my number, case you have any problems. 'Kay?" Then he pumped my hand and looked at me the same way you'd look into the casket of a loved one. "And, hey, promise me you'll call me when you finish the trail. Just so I know you're safe."

Bob then crawled into his Chrysler, gave a solemn wave, and left us standing on the sidewalk.

It took exactly eleven minutes to nearly get killed in Pittsburgh. I'm not being metaphorical.

Picture, if you will, two uncoordinated average Americans, sitting on cycling seats the size of Altoids containers, cycling through the heart of a major American city, on the shoulder of a wildly busy highway. Now imagine that it's rush hour. And pretend, for the sake of this illustration, that your hot-tempered wife is pedaling ahead of you, making your unpromising situation worse by screaming aggressively at speeding vehicles.

Urban life eddied around us. Taxi cabs. Police vehicles. Sirens. Enormous trucks. Eighteen-wheelers traveling at breakneck speeds. A BMW honked, swerving around me with a loud squeal, and I nearly quit breathing when I realized how close the vehicles came to swiping me. We had not only slipped out of our comfort zone. We had found Dante's Inferno.

It took a full fifteen minutes to pedal across our first bridge, and I was struggling to keep up with my wife's gladiatorial pace. We were on a busy three-lane highway arching over a river, cycling on a thoroughfare alongside an onslaught of speeding cars, transfer trucks, emergency vehicles, SUVs, and infuriated drivers who periodically rolled down windows and shouted mid-Atlantic obscenities at us. These vocal motorists were in for a real treat when my wife introduced all well-wishers to the Florida state bird.

Finally, we pulled over. My heart was about to pump right through my ribs and flop on the sidewalk while the math teacher consulted our pathetic paper map ($12.99). A map that should have been turned into toilet paper long ago. This was not the experience I imagined having on the GAP. I'm not sure what I expected, but this wasn't it.

The din of rush hour was too loud for my voice to be heard. But I tried anyway.

"Where are we?" I shouted.

My wife shook her head. "Can't hear you!"

"Which way are we going?"

She tapped her ear and shook her helmet.

I could tell by the way she was looking at the map that our situation was bleak. We were lost.

Meanwhile, traffic was whizzing by with wind gusts strong enough to blow off my facial features. We had no idea what exactly we were supposed to be looking for trail-wise. Where were the woods? Where was the sanctuary of nature? What about all those pictures from the guidebooks of happy people in tents, strumming Martins around campfires? How were we supposed to get to untamed wilderness from here? The only wilderness I saw within the citified hellscape was a single tree being watered by a wirehaired terrier.

Finally, my wife spotted a cop strolling by. "Oh, thank God!" she shouted, already leaping from her bike and jogging toward the man with the badge.

I pedaled behind her.

"Excuse me, Officer?" she said. "Do you know where the GAP trail starts?"

The officer started to speak, but his eyebrows rose when he saw me riding the flagship for all geriatric persons.

"What kinda bike is that?" he said.

My wife shoved the map at the officer. "Can you show me where exactly we are on this map?"

"Never *seen* a bike like that," he said, chuckling.

"It's not a bike," I said. "It's a trike."

To his credit, the officer did try to help us, but it was clear that he didn't know anything about the trail. "I'm sorry," he said. "I really can't help you. They've been rerouting the trail entrance this year, everybody keeps getting lost, and nobody seems to know where it is. I'm afraid you're on your own, guys."

"On our own?" said my wife.

"Afraid so."

And with that, Pittsburgh's Finest removed a phone from his pocket and took my picture. As he walked away, I overheard him say to his partner, "I've *gotta* get one of those for my little girl."

Jamie and I pushed our cycles to a nearby crosswalk. At the traffic light, we met a group of young men carrying large backpacks and wearing bandanas. There were four of them, and the looks on their faces were as helpless as ours. They said they had been looking for the trail for hours, consulting their maps to no avail. And I learned my first trail lesson in the bush. When you're on a pilgrimage, it is possible to build meaningful relationships based on mutual disgust. We were immediate friends.

"This is *ridiculous*," said one young man between gulps from a water bottle. "See that bridge over there? Some guy told us to go *under* that bridge, but Jack's maps say go *over* it. We can't figure out whether to go over or under or backwards."

"We coulda been halfway to DC by now," said another.

One kid tilted his map sideways. "This stupid map got four stars on Amazon."

Since my wife has always thrived during situations wherein a leader is needed, she craned her head over the young man's shoulder to observe his large atlas. Then without asking permission she commandeered his map and traced a finger over it. I could see her mind at work. She was already fitting the pieces together in her mathematical computer. Her eyes looked wild and unruly.

Somehow, being males, we all instinctively knew it would be best to remain silent and let the woman alone.

One kid leaned in and whispered to me, "Is she, like, really smart or something?"

"She has three degrees," I said.

"Three?"

I held up three fingers.

"Why?" he said.

"You're preaching to the choir, buddy."

We all remained unmoving for several minutes, watching Jamie translate markings on paper as though solving the Riemann hypothesis. Then her face suddenly brightened.

I knew that look.

She pointed forward. "Follow me," she said.

And then we were six.

The sun was setting. We had wasted an entire day looking for the trailhead. A half dozen strangers wandered through Pittsburgh on a quest to find the Three Rivers Heritage Trail, which leads to the GAP trail, with a lone math teacher leading the way. In some ways, our caravan looked downright biblical as we pedaled through the busy side streets. The map kept taking us off course, but Jamie seemed to be able to translate the map somehow, so we kept pace behind her because, truthfully, who else were we going to follow?

At times we found ourselves wandering through vacant

parking lots where a single Ford Escalade would be idling, windows tinted with roofing tar. The driver would smile at us and reveal twenty-four-carat teeth. We'd all avoid eye contact because these weren't exactly the areas of Pittsburgh where you wanted to find yourself while wearing extremely tight, asset-displaying bike shorts.

On our journey across America's sixty-eighth-largest city, more cyclists joined us. Cyclists, I discovered, tend to gravitate toward each other, especially when they're lost. Our first companion was a slender woman named Sandy on an expensive bike. She came pedaling toward us, no hands on the handlebars, carnation-white hair, and an emaciated frame.

"You guys as lost as I am?" she said.

Everyone answered in grumbling, mob-like tones.

"I've been looking all afternoon," she said, "but I can't find the trailhead. I'm so mad I could punch someone in the mouth."

She fit right in.

We had yet a few more recruits join our ranks. One was a young Russian-American man from Florida who knew exactly 4.3 words of English. Three of these words, apparently, were swear words. Another was a young guy from Nebraska on a Schwinn he bought from Walmart, which made me feel better about my own machine, which I was growing certain had been probably purchased from Toys "R" Us.

The math teacher was now leading nine people through Pittsburgh like a gaggle of confused steer, weaving through frightening mazes of skyscrapers, intersections, and sidewalks. The general consensus was, "Let's trust Jamie." I was proud of this woman, who led perfect strangers toward their destination. I only prayed she actually knew where she was going, otherwise these people might try to lynch us.

I headed up the rear of our cavalcade on my trike, riding a full three feet below everyone else's rear ends. Sidewalks led to crosswalks. Crosswalks led to empty asphalt lots, which led to detours weaving around condemned buildings and back alleys. The alleys led to more intersections, which led us beneath more behemoth bridges. We doubled back. Reoriented ourselves. Retraced our steps. Once. Twice. Three times. After hours of this, we were no closer to the trailhead than when we'd started. We picked up four more people who were also looking for the trail.

And then we were thirteen.

I have read about sailors adrift at sea, suffering the effects of malnutrition and scurvy. When they first see land, many grizzled seamen have emotional breakdowns. Some get so excited they tear off their clothing and jump right into the water, naked, swimming toward a distant shoreline. This was like that. When we found the temporary plywood ramp with a spray-painted sign reading:

GAP TRAIL

I felt like either cheering or collapsing. Or both.

The entrance to the trail couldn't have been any uglier if it had been designed by Jackson Pollock. The on-ramp was part of a construction zone, leading beneath an overpass. The trailhead was trimmed in neon cones, chain link, and orange barrels. A ramp shot downward beneath a frighteningly loud interstate where, supposedly, the wilderness began.

You could have lit the city with the looks on our faces.

We cheered loudly.

Before we parted ways, everyone paused to congratulate Jamie and slap her back. Without her, we might have ended up dead, or worse, stuck in Pittsburgh.

"Well," said Sandy, pulling on a long-sleeve racing shirt over her skeletal frame. "It's all uphill from here—literally."

"Uphill?" I said. "Really?"

"Didn't you know?" she said. "'Bout a two-thousand-foot climb uphill altogether."

"Two thousand?"

"Straight up. Ain't too bad though, if you take it slow."

"Slow. You mean like six or seven years?"

She smiled. "Don't worry, you'll be fine." She nodded to my wife. "You got a good one there. We'd all be sleeping under a bridge if it weren't for her."

"You have no idea."

We shook hands.

"Godspeed," Sandy said before releasing my hand.

Once we finished all our congratulatory remarks, we went our own ways. The last sliver of sunlight sank beneath the Pittsburgh horizon, and it was time to ride an American trail that is roughly the distance of an average Midwestern state.

The math teacher and I stood at the apex of the ramp, staring at a tiny sign that read:

WASHINGTON, DC, 350 MILES

"Here we go," said Jamie. She stepped onto her pedals and shot ahead of me, her right hand was extended in a familiar sign language gesture.

Godspeed.

# 6

*The last colors* of daylight fell upon the Monongahela River like a Monet, and I can honestly say that the Three Rivers Heritage Trail was, without question, the worst bike trail in the history of Western civilization. In fact, to call this a trail would be an insult to trails worldwide. This was a spinal injury waiting to happen.

We pedaled onward, following a paved path that was cracked and fractured with sharp humps the size of levees. I was sure that my tires or my lumbar discs were about to explode. We passed dozens of bikers undergoing the same private moments of torment. I passed one man who was sidelined, with cuts all over his body and a wet rag, stained red, held over his face. He was squatting beside his cycle, replacing a tire.

"Watch out for the potholes," he said ominously.

This sent a shiver through me. Because I immediately realized that I didn't know *how* to change a flat. Oh, I was sure I could figure it out, but the fact was, I didn't know diddly about bike gears, sprockets, derailleurs, or advanced mechanical lubrication. All I had was a single multi-tool screwdriver ($29.95) my wife bought online and a few spare inner tubes ($15.99 apiece).

The trail got worse. And the wilderness was nowhere in sight. The route carried us through industrial sections of Pittsburgh's armpit. The pavement was littered with garbage, and sometimes the trail wasn't even a trail at all, just a piece of bare ground with no clear path other than a smattering of crinkled-up cigarette cartons. We went through many areas that smelled worse than a gas station bathroom, and we passed men wearing dirty trench coats and carrying bottles in brown paper bags. Sometimes the divots in the trail were so bad the impact would knock my hat off and cause my neck to ache. We were getting the full Steel City experience.

By now I was the one in the lead, and the math teacher was following. My wife was having a harder time with the bumps than me. To take bumps on two wheels is considerably more jarring than taking them on three. On the trike, I was mostly stable, albeit uncomfortable. Jamie, on the other hand, was frequently losing her balance. Sometimes it looked like she was about to wipe out.

"You okay back there?" I'd often call out.

Then I'd hear a grunt.

After the sun disappeared, I paused on a sidewalk to let a half dozen cyclists blitz past me in the blackness. I wiped my sweaty mop with a hanky and tried to massage my trembling thighs, but it did little good to counteract the pain. My weak legs were already throbbing, and my lungs were burning something fierce. I was hopelessly out of shape, and the trail was not living up to our expectations. My wife and I thought we were going into nature, but what we got was the San Andreas Fault.

"How you doing back there?" I called out.

Grunt.

At times, the Pittsburgh portion of the trail became profoundly confusing, switching back, then forking into unmarked routes. Sometimes we thought we were on the trail; other times we were riding through—I am not kidding—a TGI Fridays parking lot. We had traveled a thousand miles to get lost in the Paris of Appalachia, and I just wanted to turn around and go home.

Then things went from bad to repulsive. I pulled over again. I crawled off my bike to catch my breath beneath a highway overpass. I took a drink from a water bottle and stretched my lower back. I shouted backward to the math teacher. "How're you doing, honey?"

But there was no grunt.

This struck me as odd. I've never known my wife to be silent.

I turned. "Jamie?"

But she was not there.

I saw a cyclist riding toward me. I stopped him and asked if he'd passed a woman about yea high, brown hair, who uses bad language.

The man braked and pointed behind himself. "Oh, yeah,

there was some woman back there who fell off her bike. Looked pretty bad."

I started running.

They were across the highway, where the trail crossed the busy road. There was a man huddled over my wife's body. I could see what had happened immediately. Jamie had skidded on the uneven pavement and was lying on her side, pinned beneath her heavy gear and her bike. And she wasn't moving.

"Jamie!"

No answer.

"Jamie!" I was nauseous.

Still nothing.

The man beside her was older, with his bike parked beside him. It looked like he was talking to her, but I could not see my wife's mouth moving. Cars sped between us.

"Is she okay?" I shouted across the highway.

He didn't acknowledge me, or maybe he couldn't hear me.

The man was pouring water on her wounds. I jogged across the road. Cars sped past me. Horns honked. I leapt out of the way of a few oncoming transfer trucks. It was like a live-action reenactment of *Frogger*.

Your mind plays horrible tricks on you when it gets scared, and my mind was doing exactly that. Fear has its own voice. *It could be a concussion. Or a broken bone. A traumatic brain injury. Dear God, don't let it be a brain injury.* I finally got close enough to hear the math teacher's voice. She was groaning. And bright blood was smeared on her thighs and forehead.

"She'll be okay," the man said. "Just took a bad fall. You really gotta watch these bumps. They're killers."

Jamie was flat on the ground, buried beneath her stuff.

She said, "I don't . . . I don't know what happened. I just . . . I just lost control."

"My son has a friend who got a concussion on this trail," said the old man. "You really gotta be careful with these bumps."

I squatted to help the man lift the heavy bike off my wife. The thing weighed more than I'd expected with all our luggage and gear.

We helped her stagger to her feet. Jamie leaned against me, and I saw the cuts and scrapes on her cheeks. There was more blood on her wrists from where she'd broken her fall. Her thighs were scraped. Her helmet was askew. Her glasses were broken. I wrapped my arms around my wife and squeezed because this was all I could think to do. I squeezed her tightly.

She winced. "Ow, that hurts." Then she whopped me.

"Where does it hurt the worst?" I said.

"I landed on my shoulder."

"How about your head?"

"I didn't hit it very hard."

"Your helmet's crooked. What if you have a concussion?"

"I don't."

We listened to cars pass like Concorde jets. I was regretting that we were here. In a way, this was all my fault. I could have put a stop to this horrible idea if I would have tried harder. I could have prevented this. We had no business being on this awful trail.

"You're bleeding pretty good," I said.

"Aw, it's not bad," said Jamie.

"Not bad?" I said. "What could be worse than bleeding?"

"Quit worrying. I'm gonna be fine. And quit looking at me like that."

"Like what?"

"Like I'm Angela Lansbury. Jeez." She buckled her chin strap, then dusted off her shorts. She climbed onto her Trek. "Are you ready to keep going or what?"

"No, I'm not ready. Look at you. You're hurt."

She shoved me then stepped onto her pedals.

"Suit yourself," she said. "I'll see you in a few weeks, butthead."

And I knew the math teacher was going to be okay.

# 7

*I once read* about an experiment wherein laboratory rats were placed in a cage with no entertainment except for a device that would deliver a painful, almost fatal electrical shock. Before the experiment, researchers hypothesized that rats would probably avoid this device after only one shock. But they were wrong. Scientists discovered that the rats would become so bored they voluntarily shocked themselves, often repeatedly, merely for entertainment value.

That's mathematics.

Mathematicians are crazy. These people aren't like you and me. I'll never forget when Jamie studied to become a math teacher. She crammed for months. Years, even. I could not understand why any sane person would willingly give up sleep to memorize things like the Pythagorean theorem, but as I say, electrical shocks.

On the morning of her certification exam, I held home-made study cards covered in Jamie's meticulous handwriting and complex formulas and quizzed her. I recited elaborate test-prep questions and listened to my wife deliver mathematical answers that sounded like Japanese to me. These were not the kinds of questions you had on math tests in third grade. "If Johnny has eighty watermelons, and you have ten . . ." No, these were questions dabbling in thermonuclear physics.

Whenever she finished answering, I would respond with either "Correct" or "Incorrect." Sometimes, for comedic value, I affected my best British game show host voice and added, *"You are the weakest link,"* just to keep things light. And that's how I lost my right incisor.

You would not believe the rigors one has to go through to teach math. It's demanding work. Teaching math is not a job; it's a lifestyle. My wife has an IQ in the quadruple digits, but passing her certification test took millions of hours of strenuous study and many late nights. I have since come to believe that the toughest creatures on the planet are certified math teachers. After our experience on the trail, I knew it was true. Math teachers are the Sylvester Stallones of the academic world.

On our first morning on the GAP trail, I awoke to discover the math teacher was nowhere to be seen. A rooster crowed. It was morning in Appalachia. The inside of our nylon dome was covered in a thin layer of dripping condensation. The rooster crowed again. I blinked several times, rifled through a few foggy memories, and tried to figure out where exactly I was and how I ended up in a tent. The night before, we had pulled over as soon as we saw the faint outlines of trees ahead and erected our tent in what we assumed was the forest. Together we fumbled with fiberglass rods and stubborn pieces of nylon until, gratefully, after what felt like hours, we successfully managed to puncture our new tent.

I sat upright. "Jamie?"

My back and legs were sore. I was stiffened by the rigor mortis that follows physical exertion, and my joints were aching.

"I'm out here," she said.

I unzipped the front tent flap and crawled outside into the cold morning air to find the math whiz making coffee on a little camp stove, fully dressed and ready for the trail. She was whistling. The blue flame was blazing against the bottom of a stainless-steel pot. She looked fresh and rested.

"I didn't think you'd ever wake up," she said.

"Is that a rooster?"

She checked her phone. "Get dressed. We're behind schedule. Time to get moving."

"I feel like I've been run over by a bus."

She probed her fresh bruises. "I'm sorry. That must be so hard for you."

Jamie handed me a tin mug. It was instant coffee with roughly the same pH rating as hydrochloric acid, only with less flavor. But it was hot, which was all that mattered. This woman was black and blue all over but somehow buzzing around our camp galley like June Cleaver.

"Who are you? And where's my wife?"

"I'm ready to get moving," she said.

"How are you feeling?" I asked.

"Fine. Mostly. It's my hands that hurt. Used this one

to break my fall. It's gone numb. I can't feel anything." She pumped her fist. "Nothing in this one either. But hey, I'm okay." She was remarkably upbeat.

"That doesn't sound good. Shouldn't we see a doctor?"

"Don't be silly. It's only a little drain bamage." She killed her coffee. "We'd better get going. Looks like rain."

"Rain."

"Lots of rain."

The sky had the pallor of a cadaver. I felt my spirits fall. I began getting dressed in the open air of Pennsylvania and decided to make a case for logic.

"Honey, nobody's making us do this, you know. You can't even feel your hands. How do you expect to grip handlebars for several hours each day? There's no shame in turning around and doing something else."

"Something else? And what exactly would *something else* be?"

"I don't know. Any activity involving beverage service."

She nodded. "Alright. Now it's my turn to ask you a question."

I slid on my shirt. "Shoot."

"How would you like scalding coffee poured down the front of those little bike shorts?"

It wasn't exactly Bogie and Bacall, but it worked. And this was when I realized, midconversation, that we were not in the woods. Not even close. We were on the outskirts of an industrial wasteland, only a few feet off the GAP trail pavement, within a far-flung suburban neighborhood.

Surrounding us were oceans of rooftops stretching toward the horizon. Behind our tent was a guy standing on his back porch, holding a mug, looking straight at me.

"Where are we?"

Jamie nodded toward the man. "His backyard."

The rooster took an encore, and we finished packing our things in under fifteen minutes.

We were off again. The man watched us leave with a ferocious scowl on his face. I could almost swear I heard the *ka-click* of a break-action coach gun behind me. This was, after all, Appalachia.

We spent the morning pedaling past train crossings, industrial places, blast furnaces, smokestacks, and neighborhoods of identical two-story houses that once formed the steel-mill villages of the Eisenhower presidency. Rain was getting closer. The sky had become aluminum gray. The worse the weather became, the faster we pedaled, although I'm not sure why we wasted our energy pedaling so ferociously. There was no way we could outrun the storm, there was no shelter in sight, and we had a lot of trail left.

In one neighborhood we passed a group of children loitering in a driveway. They watched us with great curiosity as we passed. Two little girls fell in beside us, riding pink bicycles, wearing beach ball–sized helmets and stoic faces. I could feel it coming.

"That's a dumb-looking bike," said one girl.

"Aren't you sweet?"

"Why do you ride it?"

"Because I don't wanna walk."

"Can it go fast?"

"No."

"Bet I can go faster than you."

"I have no doubt."

"I'm really fast."

"Mazel tov."

The two girls fell into a brief argument among themselves involving tales of personal athleticism until they forgot about me and started racing ahead to demonstrate their speed. When they finished their race, the girls turned around and aimed their cycles toward home, smiling when they blitzed past me.

One girl pointed to the sky and said, "You guys are about to get really wet."

"You should get a job with Channel 5."

By then, the sky had started spitting. That wouldn't have bothered me so badly if we were still living in Car World, but we lived in Bike World now. Weather, I was discovering, is a much bigger deal when you're living in a universe without the benefit of automatic windshield wipers.

Jamie and I stopped at an intersection to exchange grim looks with each other. The sky clamored with thunder every few seconds and you could feel the rumbling beneath your shoes.

"Maybe it'll blow over," I said.

"Keep thinking that," she said.

In seconds it began to rain. It was an Old Testament

torrent. The sky opened and water fell downward like someone emptying a mop bucket on our heads. Fat droplets smacked against us; shafts of water streamed from the brim of my hat. It felt like someone was tossing marbles off a balcony at us. A miniature river formed beneath our tires. There is no rain like an Appalachian rain.

We pulled beneath a shelter to don our rain slickers and cover our saddlebags with cheap plastic rain covers that turned out to be as worthless as white crayons. Here's some free trail advice: all rain gear sucks. There are no exceptions to this rule. I don't care how expensive your gear is or how many times you spray it with Scotchgard. Even the best waterproofed nylon will keep as much moisture inside as it does outside. The best way to stay dry is to go to the British Virgin Islands instead.

For hours, Jamie and I rode at a turtle's pace, thoroughly drenched, accompanied by nothing but the sound of a Niagara. We were getting cold, tired, and hungry. My wife glanced backward at me from time to time to make sure I was okay. But I wasn't. I would have rather endured a nearly fatal electrical shock.

I sat at a picnic table, dripping, shivering. I could see my breath vapor. The bedlam of rain on the picnic shelter's tin roof was akin to a truck driving through a Steinway factory. I was busy fumbling with two plastic-wrapped Swiss Rolls. The small shelter was located just off the trail, at the tail end of a rural neighborhood, and offered our only pit stop. We had been riding through the cold rain all day. My wife and I were not happy campers, literally.

The math teacher slammed her mobile phone against the picnic table and used many colorful adjectives. Her phone, which had been submerged in her "waterproof" pocket, was now dripping like a bath toy.

"Dead, dead, *dead*," she said.

Everything we owned was wet and/or dead. Our bags, our bodies, our shoes, the innermost depths of my soul. The packaged Swiss cakes were getting smashed all to heck beneath my slippery wet fingers.

"Check your phone," said the Future of Mathematics in America. "I don't even know what time it is. I can't believe my phone got wet. I paid eighty bucks for this weatherproof jacket."

I finally got the cake's plastic open. I watched with grief as one of my Swiss rolls hit the wet ground. I bent forward, reached down and wiped the gravel and Pennsylvanian slime from the violated roll, and weighed my options. On the one hand, I'm a longtime subscriber to the five-second rule. On the other, there were short curly hairs attached to this particular cake roll. Then again, I only had these two rolls left, and I was current on all my shots. I shoved the Little Debbie delicacy into my mouth.

When I unzipped my jacket pocket to check my phone, a small waterfall poured from the pocket. I removed my drippy phone, which might as well have been sitting at the bottom of a fishbowl.

Jamie plopped down beside me. "Well, turn it on."

"It won't turn on, honey. It's dead."

"Lemme see. Are you sure it's dead?"

"Deader than pleated jeans."

My eight-year-old phone had crossed the Great Divide. She fiddled with it, and I watched her get even more upset.

"You gotta be kidding me." Jamie was soon digging through our saddlebags in a veritable panic. "I hope my iPad still works, or else we'll have nothing to check Instagram."

God forbid.

I looked out at the rain while I finished my first chocolate-wrapped sponge cake. We were totally out of communication with the outside world. No texts. No GPS. No calls. No internet. No photos. I tried messing with my phone a few more times. Nothing. This is not a situation you want to be confronted with when you're a thousand miles from home with only two Swiss Rolls left to your name.

"The iPad works," Jamie said, letting the air out of her lungs. "Thank heaven. At least we can still take selfies."

"With a giant iPad? Next we'll be playing bingo and watching *Murder, She Wrote*."

She tested the device by taking what would become our first selfie on the trail. It looked like she was holding a cookie sheet in her right hand. In the photo, I don't look very happy.

And still the rain fell harder.

The rain became so loud on the sheet-metal roof that

we couldn't converse without shouting. So we simply saved our energy and sat beneath the shelter, catching our breath, watching thick quilts fall upon the mildewed homes of a faded suburbia. We stayed like that for a long while. This trip wasn't even a few days old and already one of us was beat up, with numb hands and dried blood on her thigh. The other had eaten chocolate-flavored tetanus.

"Maybe this is a sign from God," said the woman who had just unleashed a river of toe-tingling swear words. "Maybe this is actually what we need right now. To be free from our phones. To be present in this moment."

"Maybe." I opened an emergency Kit Kat bar. If this wasn't an emergency, what was?

"I mean, hey, what's the big deal about not having a phone?"

She broke a piece from my chocolate-covered wafer without asking, leaving me with dregs. She spoke with a mouthful. "Maybe we just go with it. We can always get new ones later, right?"

I didn't answer. I had given up. I had Stockholm Syndrome. I was just trying to please my captor. I nodded in agreement to satisfy her. Although she was right. We had lived most of our adulthood without smart devices. Both of us had lived gratifying lives without the benefit of technology until the world decided we needed a leash. Having no phones was no big deal. Unless, of course, we found ourselves face-to-face with the "bike path attacker."

Jamie licked her fingers. "Any more of those Kit Kats left?"

So I unwrapped another emergency Kit Kat, broke off one stick, and presented it to her. She ignored the single stick and confiscated the mother lode. She shoved the spoils of her selfishness into her mouth, all at once, without remorse.

I gazed at my boots and sighed. The paved trail lay strewn before us like red carpet, and I wasn't sure I wanted to keep going. Still, I felt myself relax a little when I noticed that the path was clearly marked now; it wasn't like we could take a wrong turn and end up in Albuquerque. We were in good health. We were together. Everyone back home knew where we were. Nobody expected anything from us, we weren't needed anywhere, we had no schedules. We had plenty of beef sticks, first-aid kits, and a waterproof toilet paper holder, for which I was suddenly very grateful. But my entire frame of mind fell into the mire when I discovered that Jamie had eaten my last Kit Kat bar.

# 8

*The inn was* a small, two-story farmhouse leaning on its side. A few shutters were falling off, and it looked like no one had cut the lawn since the Beatles broke up. I climbed onto the old porch, shook my hat dry, and rapped on the door with wet knuckles. It took about eight minutes to hear signs of life stirring in the old home. Finally, the door opened. When it did, I was immediately enshrouded in a cumulus of Kool menthol smoke.

I have a talent for finding the chain smokers.

The elderly woman at the door had fried blonde hair and was hunched at the shoulders. She was wearing a Hawaiian-print nightdress that would have qualified as a muumuu. Her cigarette had about two inches of ash on the end, and her face makeup resembled crayons left too close to a heater. I must have looked helpless and cold because after I asked about a room, her first reaction was, "You poor dears! You poor, *poor* dears. Of course we have a room. Poor dears." She said this without the cigarette ever leaving the corner of her mouth.

The inn—if that is what you called it—welcomed bikers for a meager, almost laughable fee of forty dollars a night. The good news was, we wouldn't have to sleep in our tents in the driving mid-Atlantic rain. We'd be on the second floor of an old farmhouse. The bad news was, smoke rises.

"You poor dears!" Then she barked at her husband from over her shoulder. "Harold, get out here and help these people, quick! Poor, *poor* dears."

Harold was in the back room watching *SportsCenter* at a volume loud enough to compromise dental work. Harold appeared in the doorway also accompanied by a minty cloud, wearing a plaid shirt and suspenders, with the waist of his trousers pulled up to his armpits. He brought to mind Fred Mertz after a long night.

The old woman said, "Don't just stand there, Harold! Help them. *Do something!*"

Harold shuffled onto the porch. He gave me a look. And I could see that he had Stockholm Syndrome too.

"What can I do fer ya?" he said.

"Don't just stand there, Harold. Help these poor dears with their bags and their bikes."

Harold looked at our heavy bags and grunted a bitter response. He toddled down the porch steps toward our gear and cycles, gripping the rail with both hands and wheezing.

"Come inside, you poor dears. You must be so exhausted. Right this way. You just let Harold do all the heavy lifting. Harold's a big strong man."

Harold looked to be comfortably in his late eighties.

Together Harold and I stored the heavy cycles in a dank basement beneath the dilapidated home. Then Harold and his wife showed us to our room. We found our upstairs apartment to be—I say this with the happiest of hearts—the smallest room in Pennsylvania. I have seen guest bathrooms with more square footage.

My wife and I stood in the bedroom doorway, shoeless, muscles quivering from cold, staring at a Ripley's Believe It or Not! exhibit for the world's teeniest mattress.

Once again, my wife and I spoke very few words that evening; we did not have the energy to form coherent words. Our day had been spent wading through rain, sludge, and possibly sleet. My lower body was aching in a way I have seldom experienced, with muscles twitching uncontrollably and phantom pains shooting through all major joints. Whenever I sat still for more than a few seconds, I required an enormous burst of gumption just to stand again.

We took turns showering in a clawfoot bathtub shower within a dimly lit bathroom outfitted in framed photographs of Shirley Temple and Elvis Presley. The hot water felt almost illicit when it hit my skin. I could have stayed in this shower for three years.

My wife went to bed. I did our laundry in the bathroom sink using bar soap. I hung the dripping garments over the shower curtain rod, then checked my phone again. It was totally gone.

I could hardly limp back to the bedroom without holding the wall for support. I hadn't realized how unfit I was until this moment. My body was seriously, gelatinously, out of shape.

When I opened our bedroom door, I found the math teacher already asleep, splayed on our nanomattress like a corpse. Her wet hair was fanned out on our pillows, and there were large bruises on her thighs. I kissed her neck and whispered a good night.

She flung a hand at me and connected with my jaw.

"Get off me, butthead. I'm sleeping."

Hark, fair Juliet sleeps.

I walked onto the porch to take in the chilled night and the howling Appalachian rain. After a few minutes of breathing in the saturated alpine air, I found a certain kind of beauty in this rainstorm. It sounded a lot like percussion music. In the woods, you can hear rain falling in a way that would be impossible to hear in the city. It's not just the sound that bewitches you. It's something else. It's the scent of wet rocks and foliage. It's the sound of water upon water and the occasional wind gust whipping off the hillsides to blow a fine spray into your face. It's the melody of a dripping gutter. The sound of many puddles. I cannot explain it. It's something you have to experience to know.

Then, as if God had turned off his giant faucet, the downpour began to ease, and the night atmosphere fell eerily still. Then insects began to sing. The frogs got louder. I heard the movement of unseen animals in the brush. I saw little pairs of reflective eyes looking at me. Above me, the sky turned velvet purple, and between a column of nighttime clouds, I saw the bright white moon. In the middle distance, the moonlight illuminated a range of magnificent mounded silhouettes in the darkness. I briefly wondered what these titanic shapes were until it hit me.

We were in the Allegheny Mountains.

# 9

*In 1867 a* twenty-nine-year-old man was working in an Indianapolis carriage factory when his hand slipped and he stabbed himself in the eye with a scratch awl. The young man had spent much of his youth working in sawmills, making broom and rake handles, which wasn't bad work if you could get it. But now he was blind. The injury to his right cornea was so severe that he lost vision in both eyes. Doctors said he'd probably never see again.

From his sickbed, the young man regretted that he hadn't seen half the things he wanted to see on this earth. So he made a few promises to himself, the way people often do from sickbeds. He vowed that if he ever regained sight, he would not return to factory work but would get his math teaching certification.

No, I'm only kidding. He promised that he would travel this nation on foot. And that's exactly what he did. A month later the young man's eyesight returned. Nobody could explain his recovery, and the young man didn't waste any time trying to figure it out. He simply packed a rucksack and set out from Indiana on foot. He walked approximately one thousand miles to Florida, loping across the post–Civil War South, weaving through the mountains of Kentucky, Tennessee, the Carolinas, and Georgia. His hike took place in breathtaking mountains he lovingly called the "Alleghanies." His name was John Muir.

Today, the mountains stretching from Maine to Georgia are called the Appalachians, but in Muir's day, they were the Alleghenies. The Alleghenies had become so associated with America in his era that author and historian Washington Irving once made a serious proposal to change the name of the United States to Alleghania. Irving's second choice for a national name was Appalachia.

Personally, I think this is wonderful. Can you imagine overhearing a bunch of third-graders pledging allegiance to the "United States of Appalachia"? It has a different ring to it. My uncle Tommy Lee would also be in favor of adding Dale Earnhardt to Mount Rushmore.

Today, however, the term *Alleghenies* describes only the rugged central section of the Appalachians. A portion of mountains that stretches northeast to southwest, running about four hundred miles lengthwise from north-central Pennsylvania to Virginia. At its broadest point, from east to west, the range is about a hundred miles wide. Or think of it like this: If you were to lop off the top third of North Dakota, you'd have an area about the size of the Alleghenies. Pretty dang big.

These are shallow mountains. They are not the snow-capped Rockies or the beer-commercial Tetons. For the seasoned veterans, they are like learner's permit mountains—although for a guy like me they might as well have been Denali. The highest peak in the Alleghenies, Spruce Knob, is a mere 4,862 feet above sea level. Blue Knob is a 3,000-footer. Dan's Mountain is 2,898. Savage Mountain is 2,667 feet. Meaning, most kindergarteners could do these hills on their recess breaks.

Although these hills weren't always shallow. The Alleghenies and Appalachians are old mountains, much older than the Himalayas. They were once taller than the Himalayas too. Time has worn the Alleghenies down into bare nubs compared to what they used to be, but their giant spirit is still there. And somehow, you never lose a sense of how old they are when you're among them. You can just feel it. These are not just mountains; these are upheavals formed during the Ordovician period, sometime after the birth of Cher.

One bright summer day, Jamie and I found ourselves pedaling uphill, on the gentle slopes, in perfect solitude. We were, I suppose, doing *something big*. We were accompanied by the sound of wind in trees and the scent of wet dirt. We had not passed a single person on the trail all afternoon. It was quiet. Frighteningly quiet. Horror-movie quiet. In fact, that's one of the central features of the trail: the absence of noise. You forget how accustomed you have become to the ambient sounds of traffic, distant music, or the hum of ten thousand rooftop air compressors. Pure stillness can be unsettling at first.

But after you adjust, you begin to wonder how, and why, you've gone so long tolerating a never-ending drone of static.

Now you are in earth's first cathedral, the birthplace of silence itself. Anyone who visits the woods is confronted with the fact that quietness is the natural state of the world. The world we've come to know is about as authentic as Branson, Missouri. The concrete and steel girders we live between are false. Made up. Phony. Manufactured. Temporary. Society is merely a minor interruption to all this quiet.

Let us all take a moment to reflect on how truly profound I am sounding right now.

The summer greenery hits you like an exploding public dam. You're swallowed by it. Dizzy from it. You are riding a trail lined with spruces, balsam firs, mountain ash, sugar maples, red maples, eastern hemlocks, black cherries, and American beeches. Yellow birches line your path like royal guards with swords extended.

Hardly any sunlight penetrates the thick canopy of leaves above you. This gives the feeling that you're pedaling beneath a green tarp. And the undergrowth is even greener than the umbrella above. Your whole world is green. You glance downward and see American bladdernuts, buttonbushes, Carolina roses, common elderberries, deerberries, gray dogwoods, low-bush blueberries, meadowsweets, ninebarks, purple-flowering raspberries, red-berried elders, rosebays, St. John's wort, and sweet azaleas.

Then you spot the carcass of a raccoon on the trail that is being picked apart by turkey buzzards. You smell the sacred offerings of a nearby skunk. Suddenly, the reverence is gone. Or maybe it's enhanced. Sometimes it's hard to tell.

There are so many flowers out here you can practically feel the forest procreating in front of you: marsh marigolds, barren strawberries, maple-leaf waterleaf, black-eyed Susans, monkey flowers, tall tickseed, Virginia mountain mints, white wood asters, and a bunch of other multisyllable Latin names my community-college education prohibits me from being able to pronounce. Also, there are so many pollen-producing flowers out here that if, by chance, you have seasonal allergies, you are—how should I put this?—dead.

But if I were to pick the best part of riding through the Alleghenies, it is the scents I love most. A forest will overpower you with its essence. At times, the fragrances are too much to handle inasmuch as the smells compete with one another. They come at you in waves. Sometimes you pick up the fragrance of citrus, vanilla, basil, or pine needles. Other times you smell an odor akin to cloves and cinnamon, tinged with apples. You smell leather and smoke, mud and rain. You smell the acrid bark of trees and the clean fragrance of river air. Smells get stronger and stronger until you're weary of them. They hit your lips, your tongue, the back of your throat. There is a tickle in your lungs as though you have inhaled Vicks VapoRub.

The math teacher and I broke for lunch beneath a basilica of white-barked trees. A young couple nearby were taking cell phone pictures, which is what we would have done if we'd had phones. But then it occurred to me that using a mobile phone out here only would have cheapened this experience. You cannot fit the bounty of creation into a 5.8-inch LCD screen. No, to capture all this heart-stopping beauty, you'd need at least a 9.7-inch screen.

After lunch, we followed a rickety wooden walkway down a steep mountainside to see the roaring, white-frothed Youghiogheny River, recharged from the recent rain. The river bellowed through a mountain valley, filling the world with silver mist. Neither of us broke the silence. We stood beside each other and watched. The river was loud enough to give you an earache if you stood still long enough. You could feel its bass notes reverberating in your belly. The word *Allegheny* is a Lenape word that means "fine river." What a fine river it was.

I have lived the majority of my adult life snug in the lap of strip malls, Whataburgers, Home Depots, and Best Buys. I am like most suburban guys, wholly dependent on T.J. Maxx. But I was feeling a bit of regret out here, regret that I had deprived myself of the basic human right of being outside.

Before I became a writer, I used to work outside for a living. I crawled upon pine-framed homes and had a winter tan. My red hair was always bleached. What had happened to me? Such is the life of a writer. And I guess I've adapted to it. The rural child within me had been starved unto death and was quietly replaced with a middle-aged man who was hopelessly addicted to Cinnabon. I had passed entire eras beneath fluorescent lighting, staring at a single monitor, writing words instead of living them. Well, all I can say for myself is, poor dear.

"Hey! I just killed a spider!" shouted the math teacher, holding a giant beef stick like a weapon.

She swatted again.

"I just got two more!"

*Swat, swat, swat.*

"Six spiders!"

Our campsite for the evening was an overgrown, weed-infested hellhole that hadn't been well maintained since the Punic Wars. There were spiders everywhere. These were not your common household spiders either. These were spiders with postpubescent body hair.

Between swats, the math teacher admired her kill. "Ooh, look at that one. He was huge." More swats. "Look at the mess *he* made!"

How wonderful.

I was beginning to feel nauseous.

Earlier, I had attempted to visit the campground privy, which turned out to be an arachnid singles bar. The northern black widow is native to Pennsylvania. So is the brown widow, the woodlouse hunter spider, the brown recluse, and Kevin Bacon. I was prepared to hold my bladder until we got back to Florida.

I unpacked our saddlebags and began preparing supper on our temperamental cookstove. I started boiling water in a pan, opening boxes, and consulting the culinary instructions of Uncle Ben. The math teacher took out another battalion of rebels and said, "Hurry up with that rice. Killing spiders is making me hungry."

Several other campers were pitching tents nearby under a peach-colored dusk. Among them was the slender woman we'd met in Pittsburgh, Sandy. She was erecting a small single-person tent. She moved with the relaxed mannerisms of a woman who had done all this outdoor business before. You can spot the trail veterans. They aren't like the rest of us. Trail veterans are the ones who don't bother killing the spiders.

Sandy's snug-fitting activewear revealed a body so gaunt that it was almost hard to look at. She had the look of either an athlete or someone who was sick. I couldn't tell which.

"You made it, Sean," she said.

I couldn't believe she remembered my name. "We made it."

"So," she said, "how's the Dynamic Duo this evening?"

"Tired and sore."

"Yeah, well, trust me, you'll sleep like a baby tonight."

"You mean I'll wake up every hour and cry?"

"Pretty much."

We were suddenly interrupted by a large group of youthful campers who arrived on electric bikes. Sandy rolled her eyes when she saw their machinery. "Oh, brother. Here come the Hondas," she said.

The GAP caters to a lot of electric bikes. Some days, it seemed like most of the bikes we passed were electrified. Many trail purists do not care for the new phenomenon of battery-powered machines since these bikes go against the original idea of the trail and open the virginal wilderness to people who otherwise would not have been there. Namely, party animals.

Our new neighbors were a prime example. They were in their early twenties, loud, and bursting with hormones. These newcomers were soon joined by more friends on electrified bikes, their feet weren't even touching the pedals. Our campground was quickly becoming a glorified frat party. Soon there were a few dozen battery-powered bikes corralled around our campsite. Young men walked around shirtless in swim trunks, poking out their chests in a manner that made my lower back hurt to watch. And although we were having unusually cold weather, all the young women were wearing bathing suits that looked like strategically positioned Band-Aids.

Sandy shook her head. "Don't know where they plan on swimming. The Yough's cold enough to freeze your butt."

"Something tells me they aren't interested in aquatic sports."

She shrugged. "Well, I say God bless 'em. But I'm not doing mouth-to-mouth unless it's one of the cute guys."

After supper, sine waves of hormonal energy were crashing against our tent. The young folks had positioned their tents in a large semicircle, and in the time-honored tradition of all college kids, they began blaring music from a loudspeaker. Our tranquil campsite had been transformed into the Kappa Alpha social club.

Late that night, I stepped outside the tent to "see a man about a dog," and I found Sandy staring at the sky in a kind of forlorn trance, wholly unbothered by the noise. She sat on the picnic table, legs crossed lotus style. I sat beside her as "Brown Sugar" played on the kids' stereo system. There was something about this woman that made me wonder if everything was okay.

Sandy looked at me with a smile and pointed upward. "You ever seen so many stars?"

I looked into the sky. Until that moment, I hadn't actually noticed the stars. I was too busy shoving wads of toilet paper into my ears. But she was right. The view was incredible. It looked like God had freshly painted the fabric of heaven.

"I wish I woulda brought earplugs," I said.

"I have spares if you need." She reached into her pocket and handed me plastic-wrapped plugs.

"Thanks."

She nodded to our friends. "If I woulda known we were attending a Stones concert, I woulda brought my BIC."

"Yeah, well, I wish they'd at least have the decency to play some Skynyrd."

Our friends got drunker, louder, and cackled harder. They hocked loogies and chased each other. They made explosive bodily noises that could be heard across state lines. They carried on enlightening conversations. I noticed a girl passed out, lying facedown on the bare ground, limbs splayed in awkward directions. It was shocking, and I thought she was hurt since she wasn't moving, but amazingly, she managed to keep drinking beer.

I wanted to have a more in-depth conversation with Sandy, but I was too tired. It was almost 2:00 a.m., and the revelry was too loud for me to concentrate. I wished her good night and left her to her sky watching.

When I arrived back at our tent during a screaming lead guitar solo, my wife was awake from the noise. She rubbed my tense shoulders and said in a groggy voice, "What song is that?"

"'War Pigs.'"

"Where were you?"

"Meeting the neighbors."

Jamie moved her hand to my hair and rubbed my scalp. "Just get through tonight. We'll never see these obnoxious kids again."

"Is that a promise?" I wedged a plug into my ear canal.

The math teacher made large circular motions in my hair. They were soothing. After a few minutes, I was beginning to doze into the pleasant pastures of dreamland when I felt her hand abruptly stop. I heard her jump. My eyes flicked open to see Jamie huddled against the tent wall with wide eyes, a beef stick cocked behind her head like a baseball bat.

"Hold very still," she said.

My screams could be heard for miles.

The morning arrived with the sounds of birds. Lots of birds. You cannot imagine how many birds are in the Alleghenies. More than 200 species of native birds are found in the Allegheny National Forest, and 199 of them were outside our tent. This was their peak migration season. There were ospreys, herons, and ruffed grouse within plain view. When I stepped out of my tent to greet the morning, I saw a lone bald eagle flying overhead, gliding upon the cold morning air. I had never seen a bald eagle before.

The bluish early light made the woods look haunting, and the dew made the air smell brand new. Surprisingly I felt refreshed, considering how little sleep I'd gotten the night before.

Sandy and I were both packing our campsites into tiny bags, then placing these bags into other larger bags, which would then be crammed into even bigger bags, before finally being attached to our cycle frames. Jamie was down on the banks of the Yough River, washing her hair.

I asked Sandy the most common question on the trail.

"How many miles you doing today?"

The slender woman cinched a strap on her saddlebags. She looked off into the forest. "I'll just ride until I can't. That's normally how I do it. I don't like to plan. I usually just disappoint myself."

She was being modest. I could tell by the woman's cycling attire she was not merely a hobbyist biker. Her bike looked like it cost more than a tactical government helicopter.

"I don't believe you." I nodded to her bike. "Are you a competitive cyclist or something?"

"Or something."

She folded her tent into a tiny ball, then placed it into an airtight sack.

"I used to compete," she said, "but not anymore. I wasn't

any good anyway. What about you? How far are you guys riding today?"

"No idea. My knees went to be with Jesus after the first hour."

"Just wait." She pointed toward the mountains. "Next, Jesus is gonna take your thighs."

I laughed. But not that hard.

It's bizarre how close you feel to strangers on a trail. You don't experience this kind of comradery in the real world. You go to a supermarket and people give you dirty looks if you forget to use one of those divider thingies on the checkout conveyor belt. But out here, you're on the same team. People share food, supplies, water, and stories. You are all going through the same weather, the same hills, the same crises, the same terrain, the same mechanical problems. You are all, let's face it, on the same path. I don't mean to sound this wise, it just comes naturally.

"It'll get easier," said Sandy, who was inspecting her bike, doing a preflight check. "Your legs will get stronger once you settle into a rhythm. Few more days, you'll be a pro, and you won't want it to end. It's like that for everyone. The trail sort of makes you stronger."

"I don't think it's working on me."

She paused to stretch her knees. Her upper thighs were about as wide as my forearms. "Give it time."

One of the sleeping young people nearby let out a loud snore, then rolled over. I wanted nothing more than to forget the previous night's tribute to Black Sabbath. I glanced at a young man's feet dangling from an unzipped tent. There were aluminum cans strewn on the ground and a prodigious smattering of cigarette butts.

Sandy laughed. "Those are some legendary livers."

"Did you get *any* sleep last night between guitar solos?"

"Some. I think I fell asleep somewhere between Joe Walsh and AC/DC. But I was up late anyway, watching the stars."

"You must be a cheap date."

"I've never seen so many stars. You can't see them like that where I live."

"And where's that?"

"New York. Live right outside the city, in Red Hook."

"Long way from home."

She nodded. "I can't remember the last time I saw the Milky Way. Maybe Girl Scouts. I musta been ten or eleven. You forget about stuff like that when you get older."

This woman was becoming a minor mystery to me. I asked another common question and hoped to get more information. "So what made you do the trail?"

The woman did not respond for a few moments, and when she did her answer was cryptic. "Well . . . let's just say I have a lot going on right now."

And that was that.

I let it die. None of my business.

Whole minutes piled up between us while we continued shoving bags into other bags, and still more bags, like Russian dolls from hell. Without looking up from her busy-work, Sandy said quietly, "Breast cancer."

She stopped packing and said it again plainly. No emotion. "I have breast cancer."

I wasn't sure exactly how I was supposed to respond. How do you respond? I looked at her and felt bad for having asked the question that led us here. She was probably out on this trail to forget such things, and here I was probing the wounds.

"It's kinda bad," she said.

I said nothing.

"My doctor says if you get breast cancer, this is not the kind you want to get." She laughed. "What can I say? Lucky me."

It felt like someone had delivered a gut kick to us both. I only wish I could have taken back the question and started this entire morning over.

"The worst part ain't the cancer or the radiation," she said. "It's not the meds either, although those are no fun. You know what it is? It's being afraid. You're always battling fear, not the cancer. Even when you sleep, you're doing battle against fear. That is, if you *can* sleep. Which you usually can't.

"You wake up each morning and keep fighting fear. You never get a break, you're always freaked out, your adrenal glands are always pumping, you can't think about anything else. Sometimes I think it woulda been better just not knowing, and—" She stopped midsentence. "Anyway . . . I figured it was time to get out here and live. I'm tired of being afraid. I can still move my body, so that's what I'm doing. Moving."

"Are you winning the fight?"

Shrug.

"Sometimes I think yes. Other times . . . I dunno. My daughter's taking it a lot worse than I am. As a parent it makes it worse seeing your kids get scared. They have their own fear to deal with. The only thing worse than dying is watching someone else die."

I wanted to ask more questions. I wanted to know how this sick woman had the fortitude, let alone physical stamina, to ride a four-state trail. Above all, everything in me wanted her story to have a happy ending. But that's not how life works.

"I'm a single mom. I'm all she has left. When I'm gone—" Again she stopped. We had entered new conversational territory.

"Where does your daughter live?"

"New Hampshire."

I nodded.

"She's actually picking me up in Georgetown when I'm done with the trail in Virginia. Can't wait to see her. She's my life."

This signaled the end of our exchange.

We hadn't traveled all these miles to wallow in anxiety and sadness. She'd had enough of that already.

Thankfully, we were then interrupted when one of the young campers stirred in his tent. A young man stood, massaged his temples, staggered to a clearing, lowered his waistband, and Sandy and I both heard the unmistakable noise of a healthy urethral system at work. Sandy began to laugh. And I did too. This little break in the solemnity was a minor gift.

She jerked her head at the kid. "Well, at least he has the decency to keep his back to us."

"What a gentleman."

"I wouldn't mind being that age again."

"You couldn't pay me enough."

"You won't be saying that after the hills today, honey."

Sandy smiled and mounted her bike. She buckled her helmet and gave me a two-fingered wave. There were deep creases in her cheeks and lines around her eyes. "You ever seen the Milky Way before?" she said.

"Been a long time."

"Well, here's a word of advice: don't miss it."

Sandy stood on her pedals and lowered her shades.

"Take care," she said.

"Godspeed," said I.

*10*

*Try this. Imagine* a lonesome trail hugging a mountain bend, leading you into 20,633 acres of hardwood forest. Now imagine a fourteen-mile river gorge running directly through the center of this pine-scented haven. Imagine waterfalls that drop ten, twenty, and thirty feet into the Youghiogheny River—not just one or two, but multitudes, with names that are almost as wonderful as the falls themselves: Cucumber Falls, Meadow Run Waterslides, and Sugar Run Falls. Imagine the exposed sides of granite mountains, towering above you. Now imagine that you are seeing all this from eye level, with nothing to serenade you but the sound of your own frantic, pathetic breathing as you pedal onward beneath the failing strength of your scrawny, pale chicken legs.

When we reached Ohiopyle State Park, my wife was pedaling in the lead, admiring such overlooks with one finger on her handlebars. Meanwhile, I was sucking wind. My wife and I were on opposite ends of the physical-fitness spectrum. She had grown more confident on her bike with each mile, and now, from my angle, she looked like she'd been born on the thing. Her knees had become super pistons with minds of their own. She could have pedaled and read the paper at the same time if she'd wanted. Whereas I was riding several hundred feet behind her, about eye level with her knees, struggling to keep up. My daily view consisted of Jamie's backside, cruising far ahead of me. Often she would glance back at her poor husband, pedaling as fast as he could but lagging behind, and she'd flash a woeful smile as if to say, "I should have married the quarterback."

"Keep pedaling!" she would call out to me.

Ohiopyle State Park, considered by trail goers to be the highlight of the GAP trail, is home to the Ferncliff Peninsula, a 100-acre National Natural Landmark with a warmer microclimate inside the river canyon, which allows unique plant specimens to survive in mini ecosystems. Simply put, this place is a world of its own. It's not like the rest of the GAP. It has a florid feel that you won't get anywhere else.

Once upon a time, this peninsula was a wildly popular tourist destination. There were quaint hotels and camps, painted fences, gazebos, bowling alleys, and fine restaurants. The old Ferncliff Hotel was king of the heap—a fifty-room Victorian inn with enough rocking chairs on the porch to make a Cracker Barrel jealous. Ohiopyle was not just a resort. It was *the* resort of the mid-Atlantic. Pre–Henry Ford, people paid one dollar to ride the Western Maryland rails to get here and spend a few weeks doing nothing but playing shuffleboard, waltzing, reading novels, and knocking down the pins. This place would have hosted spring formals in dancing pavilions with cocktail lights stringing above the forest. There would have been string quartets playing Schubert, young women in voluminous skirts with crinolines, and large bowls of red rooster punch strong enough to remove paint from Navy ships. It would have been charming.

But then along came the automobile.

Everything died. The age of the Model T stunted the attention span of the American family. Families no longer wanted sleepy resorts playing Schubert. They wanted road trips. They wanted to stay in Wigwam motor inns and eat onion rings at truck stops. By the 1940s, this resort was officially in the grave. Ohiopyle became a hazy memory. Today, Ohiopyle is all forest. When you look at it, you would never guess there had ever been anything there except poison ivy.

A behemoth wood and iron bridge carried my wife and I over the Yough River Gorge—Pennsylvania's deepest. We peered over the side of the rail and found ourselves staring downward at rocks and rushing currents. The repurposed railroad bridge launches cyclists over some of the most thrilling views found on the GAP. They were some of the best views I had ever seen, period.

It was a marvelous day to be in the woods. And everyone else in the tricounty area thought so too. Ohiopyle Park was slammed. This was the first time we had seen the trail this busy, and it was startling at first. It hadn't taken long to get used to solitude. We were constantly dodging traffic in the form of pedestrians, other cyclists, and walking teenagers who were all—and I mean every last one of them—staring at their phones. I might not have noticed this had I not been going through severe phone withdrawal.

We were continually dinging our bells at phone users and announcing, "Coming through!" But very few people seemed to notice us or hear our heated dinging. Every couple of yards we were averting serious collisions with people who were spellbound by glowing screens.

I saw one guy standing in the center of the bridge, thumbing away on an iPhone when a pack of professional-looking cyclists thrummed by him traveling upwards of thirty miles per hour. They knocked him off balance, and the man landed on his rump. He blurted an ugly word to the bikers. The bikers cussed back at him. And the remarkable thing about all this is, not once during this altercation did the man ever stop tweeting.

My wife dinged her bell at a group of teenagers.

"Watch out! Coming through!"

The teenagers clogging the path gave my wife that apathetic look that only teenagers know how to make. "How about *you* watch out, lady?" one kid said.

This poor adolescent was not prepared for the certified math professional to pump her brakes, dismount, and stare him in the eyes. I could swear I heard the gentle sound of something solid filling that poor kid's drawers.

"I said," the math teacher began slowly, "you'd better *watch out*." Her voice was barely above a whisper.

He stepped aside.

The final straw came, however, when we were nearly flattened by two passing cyclists wearing hemp-weave clothing and Birkenstocks. These bikers were tapping on phones *as they pedaled*, which we'd been told was becoming a common cause of injury on the trail. There are horror stories about phone users on the GAP who have sustained serious brain trauma because of texting and pedaling. Personally, I don't know how anyone could travel at high speeds and check TikTok at the same time. But I promise you, people do it.

The average American spends five hours per day on a phone, checks their phone between forty and a hundred times per day, sends 2,819 texts per month, and touches their phone an average of 2,167 times per day. Seventy-one percent of Americans admit to sleeping beside their smartphones. Fifty-two percent of teens admit to playing on smartphones while hanging out with friends in absolute silence. Eighty percent of users admit to occasionally texting while driving. Right now, as you read this, 660,000 people are engaged on their phones while behind the wheel. And here's the truly chilling statistic: the average American will spend eleven years of their life span on a smartphone.

Eleven years.

But that's enough depressing stats for one chapter. By the time Jamie and I approached Ohiopyle proper, the trail opened up a little and we were pedaling at a good pace again, admiring the magnific views. Also, there was an alarming new development in my life. No sooner were we approaching the train depot visitor center than my gears began making noise. Serious noise. My trike started to grind loudly, attracting the stares of nearby cyclists. The shrill crunching of gears gave way to mechanical scraping. Scraping gave way to popping. All of a sudden, I was locked in the trike's most difficult gear setting, thrusting my legs against extreme resistance as though pedaling the USS Wisconsin uphill. Everyone was watching me with amused stares.

I called to Jamie, who was a few hundred feet ahead.

"Hey! Something's wrong with my bike!"

"What?"

"Wait up! My bike! I think it's broken!"

"Don't you mean trike?"

Everyone's a smart aleck.

"Stop pedaling!" I said.

She skidded to a stop and narrowly avoided wrecking with a convoy of cyclists in matching jerseys. She turned back just in time to see my unique piece of three-wheeled idiocy shed several bolts and springs. The metallic clanging on the pavement was accompanied by the vision of random bits of steel hardware bouncing across the path. Nuts and screws spewed behind me like confetti. And this being the Land of the Free, Home of the iPhone, everyone got the whole thing on video.

## 11

*The birds were* chuckling. The insects were howling. You could hear the faint song of the river moving through the mountains. In the distance, I could see Ohiopyle's lone beer-and-burger joint alive with nightly tourist customers. Small groups of middle-aged people in Lycra were laughing loudly, their voices echoing throughout the mini village. Everyone seemed so happy. But I felt no cheer.

Welcome to the borough of Ohiopyle. Population thirty-six. Our boarding house looked like an Andrew Wyeth painting at sunset, the farmhouse framed by distant high-lands straight out of a Whitman poem. But I was not in the mood to enjoy it.

I was lying on my back, attempting to fix my trike with a cheap multi-tool. The trike was parked on the porch of our boarding house. Grease covered my hands. I turned the wrench between periodic sips from a sweaty Michelob bottle. It was the first beer I'd had since the pandemic began.

We hadn't planned to stay in Ohiopyle, of course. But then again, I hadn't planned on witnessing my trike mechanically explode either. My machine was in bad shape. I knew it had something to do with the derailleur, but truthfully, I wasn't quite sure what a derailleur was, or how this cycle part differed from, say, a desk lamp.

I finally gave up and threw my wrench against the porch floorboards because, let's face it, I had no idea what I was doing down there. I'm not completely useless when it comes to mechanics. I once worked as an electrician's assistant. But I was helpless in the face of a tricycle.

I sat on the steps, peeling the Michelob label with my thumbnail, feeling sorry for myself. I have my black belt in self-pity. The fun was officially over. There was a lot of trail ahead of us, and I would have to either walk home or call an Uber. Did they even have Uber in these parts? Probably not. So scratch the Uber idea. I would have to find a mule train to take us home.

The math teacher appeared in the doorway. Her hair was wet, and she was wearing a towel turban. I wonder who teaches women to make those.

"Did you fix it?" she said.

"Nope. Actually, I think I'm making it worse. I think the frame is bent."

"Bent?"

"Bent."

"Think you can figure it out?"

"Nope."

Jamie lifted the longneck from my hand and took a sip without asking. A healthy sip. She steals.

"Well, don't give up yet," she said. "It'll still be here in the morning."

"I sincerely hope it's not."

She handed me her empties and then touched my face. "Let's sleep on it before we start making any big decisions. Take a shower. Rest." Then she walked inside, leaving me to grieve my half-dead Michelob.

That night we slept with the bedroom windows open so that we could hear the forest come to life around us. One thing I've learned about camping is that it's far more enjoyable when you're lying on a Tempur-Pedic mattress in a boarding house with the windows open.

I inhaled the refrigerated night air and glanced at the heavy packs beside my nightstand. I should have been happy about the possibility of our trip being finished; I hadn't wanted to do this stupid trail in the first place. But oddly, I didn't want to quit. I didn't want to leave the trail half finished. I liked being out here. My, how quickly we change! I liked being in the woods with no schedules to keep, with nobody expecting anything of me. I liked living from meal to meal. Out here, I was phone free for the first time in I can't remember how many years. No phone ringing, no notifications, no constant stream of text conversations, no robocalls with important information regarding my auto manufacturer's warranty. I didn't want to go back to just cutting the grass and paying the insurance.

I fell asleep, serenaded by the soprano section of crickets, with the warm body of my wife huddled beside me. We slumbered beneath thick comforters that smelled like laundry detergent. I had the best sleep I'd had in years.

I awoke early. The world was still dark when I wandered down the narrow staircase to make coffee in the communal Mr. Coffee machine. A little label on the coffeemaker read:

CLEAN THE COFFEEMAKER WHEN
FINISHED. I AM NOT YOUR MOM. THX.

When I emerged onto the back porch holding a hot cup, I inhaled the steam into my nose and tried to temporarily forget our predicament. I looked at the morning sky and searched for the stripe of the Milky Way like Sandy said, but saw nothing.

Then I heard voices.

The voices were male. They were coming from the front of the house. I heard light laughter, followed by the sound of clinking metal.

I walked around the clapboard structure, barefoot in the grass, and was greeted by a cumulus of butterscotch-smelling vapor that hit me like a fog machine. Two men were speaking to each other quietly, interrupted only by the rhythmic ratcheting of a socket wrench. I knew that sound. I grew up with that sound. My father worked on cars every weekend of his life and changed his oil every nine-point-two miles.

There was an old man lying on the pavement beneath my trike, working with a headlamp and a wrench. A small set of tools lay scattered on the pavement beside him.

His friend was sitting on a bench and saw me approach. "Morning." He was old too. All freckles, with red hair that had refused to go white.

"If you guys are gonna steal my trike," I said, "you're gonna need a few bucks for cab fare."

The man on the ground ratcheted a few more times. He had white hair and wore Teddy Roosevelt glasses.

"No way," he said. "Bike thievery is a hanging offense in these parts. We wouldn't do that to you."

"I promise to look the other way just this once."

He stopped ratcheting, laughed, and took a hit from his vapor pen.

See, what did I tell you? Smokers.

"We saw you come in last night," he said. "Noticed your machine was worse for the wear, thought maybe we could help."

I didn't know what to say, and I could hardly believe this was happening. You're never prepared for the little acts of kindness that happen to you personally. You read about them all the time, but when you are the recipient, things feel differently. The little skeptic inside you just won't die, and you keep wondering why someone would be so considerate. I felt a little embarrassed accepting charity from two old men. These guys were complete strangers and old enough to be my grandfathers.

"Where you from?" I said.

The redhead spoke. "Brick Township."

"He don't know where that is," said the old man turning the wrench. "We're from New Jersey."

"The Garden State," I said.

"No," said the man beneath the bike. "More like the Toll Booth State."

"You're a long way from home."

"Thank the Lord."

I waited for the discussion to pick up momentum, but it never did. They seemed content to remain quiet and revel in their miasma of butterscotch. The old man worked. The redhead looked at the stars. Nobody asked where I was from or what my name was. So I let my IBS (Incessant Baptist Speaking) of the mouth fill in the gaps. I don't even remember what I was talking about. All I can remember was finally managing to say, "I don't know how to thank you, sir."

"And you don't have to," he said.

I could see a smear of black chain lubricant across his cheek.

"Gotta look out for each other, right?" he added.

"That's right," said his friend. "We have to start asking ourselves, what kind of a world are we gonna leave behind for Willie Nelson?"

"You a bike technician or something?" I asked.

The redhead shook his head and said in a whisper, "He's a priest."

The old man beneath the trike gave a hoarse laugh. He slapped my recumbent seat. "Yeah, but I don't usually do exorcisms. Looks like you ran this machine through a trash compactor. Your derailleur is torn up. And see this little piece of your frame? It's bent. What happened there?"

"I don't know. Is it fixable?"

He went back to work. "Well, let's just say the jury's out."

It took about twenty more minutes for the old man to finish half repairing the pathetic excuse for machinery by beating it with a hammer and doing a lot more ratcheting. When he was finished, I didn't know what to say, so I didn't say anything more than thank you.

"Well, this is about the best I could do for you under the circumstances," the padre finally said, putting the tools away. "Try not to let it fall apart on me, okay? Bad for business."

He washed his hands at a nearby hosepipe and said, "You'll wanna keep an eye on that derailleur. It's pretty chewed up. And that frame is weakened in the place where I bent it back into its original shape."

"You know a lot about bikes for a priest."

"Used to be a mechanic in a previous life. Bikes are easier than cars. And they're a *lot* easier than people." He smiled. "Go ahead, test it out. Let's see how she runs."

I crawled onto the seat and pedaled in circles around the lawn. They cheered for me. I felt pretty silly, getting so excited about a repaired tricycle, but I was cheering too.

Afterward, we all shook hands and I watched as the padre and his partner cinched the straps on GE refrigerator–sized backpacks. The old man took a draw of butterscotch and the vapor wafted through his nostrils as he faced the immense, towering wilderness before us.

I asked where their bikes were.

"No bikes," said the redhead. "We're walkers."

"That's why we gotta hurry," said the padre. "We wanna make Rockwood by dark."

Rockwood was at least thirty miles away.

"On foot?" I said.

He sighed and gazed into the outlying mountains. "I picked quite a week to quit smoking, didn't I?"

"So wait, let me get this straight. A *priest* fixed your bike?" My wife pedaled beside me in the cool morning on an empty trail. The conifers whipped past us as we coasted on a brief downhill. The scent of soggy earth was overwhelming.

"That's what he said. And it's a trike, not a bike."

My machine was working much better than it had the night before. It was still making noise, but the noises sounded less fatal. I would survive. Together we pedaled along a stretch of heart-stopping Pennsylvanian wilderness in pure quiet, serenaded by magpies and starlings and my demoniac derailleur. The morning sky was the color of peach sherbet—the kind of sherbet you can't buy in the grocery store. The clouds were purplish. It really was quite a morning.

"A *priest*," she said. "With the collar and everything?"

"He was just wearing a T-shirt."

My wife was pumping her legs and eating a CLIF Bar.

"Did you have to call him Father and all that?"

"No. But he did have one of those e-cigarettes."

"Shut *up*. He was vaping?"

"Yep."

"Are priests allowed to do that without going to, whadd-ayacallit . . . purgatory?"

I shrugged. My policy is to leave theological discourse to experts.

My father raised me as a deepwater Baptist, whereas he began his life as a staunch German Catholic. He came from a Kansas town with a three-page phonebook. He was schooled by nuns, played baseball on a team coached by priests, and was an altar boy. My father spoke Latin. Still, Catholicism was something he never talked about. Not even once.

Long after he died, I had been going through some old boxes in my mother's attic when I'd found a small wax candle and an infant christening gown packed tightly in a shoe-box, wrapped in plastic. I asked my mother about it, and she explained that my father's German parents insisted I get baptized in the Roman Catholic Church. So my father had me baptized to appease them. Or more specifically, to appease his own guilt. Catholics, my mother told me, have a corner market on guilt.

I'm not so sure about that. Baptists don't even wave at each other in the liquor store.

This news was earthshaking for me. "Are you telling me that I'm Catholic?" I asked my mother. "Heaven's no," she said. "You're not Catholic; you're going to heaven."

After that, I became mildly fascinated with the Catholic tradition. I began looking into it out of curiosity, hoping it would reintroduce me to a dead man. I visited Catholic churches anonymously. I even went to confession a few times.

"You know something?" The math teacher was riding hands-free now. "I've never even been to a Catholic church."

"Yeah, well, if you enjoy foreign movies without subtitles, you'll love it."

She pulled alongside me. "This is a sign, you know. You realize that. This is your sign."

"You think everything is a sign."

She shrugged. "He was *Catholic*."

"Do you realize how many Catholics there are in the world?"

"Counting you?"

"Stop it."

"Well, you are."

I am not Catholic, of course. Not even close. I don't exactly know what I am, but I know that you do not merely shed your childhood beliefs so easily. No matter what you find in a shoebox. My parents made me what I am, whatever that may be.

Then again, if our childhood beliefs shape us, then what about my father's childhood beliefs? How could he leave his Catholic upbringing behind and go full-tilt Oral Roberts?

"Catholics can drink," my wife said. She flipped her bike into a lower gear. "So I guess they can smoke too. I wonder about gambling."

"Catholics are allowed to gamble."

"We should totally convert."

If you ever hear that I've filed Chapter 11, it will be because of my wife's affection for a game called Buffalo Gold, found at the Beau Rivage in Biloxi.

After I'd learned about my newfound Roman Catholic affiliation, every year on the anniversary of my father's death I would attend a Catholic mass. I chose a different chapel each year. I'll never forget the first time I attended as an adult. It was a vibrant experience. And completely alien to me. I was reared beneath the teachings of George Beverly Shea and Gloria Gaither. I had no idea what to make of statuary, votives, and liturgy.

One of the hardest facets about Catholicism for me to swallow was that many Catholics believe that all suicide victims went to hell. My father's own family believed this. This is partly why his family disowned us after his funeral. I never knew his parents. There were no gray areas in the minds of my father's parents where hell was concerned. My father was burning. I heard it from their own mouths. And then I never saw them again.

Even so, I'd found a beauty in the ceremony of mass. And I will forever recall a wrinkled woman who sat in the pew next to me, praying fervently in another tongue. We sat beneath an arresting stained-glass window portraying the Madonna as I listened to her talk to God. It was like nothing I'd ever experienced before. And it felt almost scandalous to my fundamentalist brain. For crying out loud, my mother's Bible study met on Wednesdays specifically to pray against Madonna.

After pedaling for a few hours in quiet, I noticed a huge vaporous cloud rising from the heads of two hikers ahead on the trail.

"That's them," I said, pointing.

"Who?" said Jamie.

"The priest."

We pedaled hard until we overtook the two men. They were smiling and waving at us. The padre gave me a thumbs-up and said in a strong Jersey accent, "Looks like your machine's holding up. You must have one heck of a good mechanic, pal."

I dinged my bell to show appreciation. "If this thing falls apart on me, I'm filing a complaint with the pope."

"Get in line," he said.

"I could never thank you enough."

"I told you, it was nothing."

"I thought priests weren't supposed to lie."

"No comment."

We laughed a little, talked some more, and then I bid the two old wayfarers goodbye. I left them with my new favorite word, which seemed to genuinely please the old man, who probably knew what the term meant. "Godspeed," they both responded. It made me feel very Catholic.

The math teacher and I pedaled onward wearing smiles. It was a Monday. A perfect September Monday. And it was the twenty-sixth anniversary of my father's suicide. Maybe it was a sign.

## 12

*The human butt* can only take so much. You cannot imagine how bruised the rear feels after being viciously smashed, squished, bounced upon, and repeatedly abused for days at a time. If you think I'm exaggerating, then you have never mistreated your fundaments as I have. Traditional cycling saddles were apparently designed by masochists who were missing their reproductive organs and had tiny derrieres. The pain is worse than you think. Some cyclists on the trail are unable to tough it out. One of the most common causes for people quitting the trail is pain in the buttocks and in the crotch. There is no such thing as a comfortable saddle. Mankind's (and womankind's) haunches were not meant to ride any kind of cycle—let alone a trike. Every man has his breaking point. I had reached mine.

"My butt hurts," I said.

"You complain more than anyone I know."

I shifted in my seat. "Well, it does."

"That's because you're riding a toy."

"Which you bought for me."

"Because you're *afraid of bikes*."

We were approaching a wooden sign announcing the turnoff for the nearby community of Confluence.

"Let's stop here," I said.

"You seriously wanna stop? We can still fit in a few more miles before it gets dark."

"Who are we trying to impress? Plus, they have a grocery store here."

She braked and faced me. "Do you ever think about anything but Swiss Rolls?"

"Sometimes Chick-fil-A."

The borough of Confluence looks like Mayberry. It is located at the southern end of the Lower Turkeyfoot Township. The community hugs the bottom of Pennsylvania like a flea hanging from a dog's belly, about ten miles from the Maryland border. Here, the Casselman River, Laurel Hill Creek, and the Youghiogheny River join each other in a convergence, thus the name.

You can see the rivers meeting beneath you while riding across a deck plate and girder bridge that leads you off the GAP and into the town. You will find random cyclists stopped on this bridge, impeding the flow of trail traffic, taking in the view, without regard for others. You will be one of these annoying people. Because it's a killer view.

Pennsylvania's highest point, Mount Davis, is nearby. And just down the road from Confluence is the immense Youghiogheny River Lake, a flood control reservoir where bass boats and anglers gather each weekend to partake in a wide variety of Anheuser-Busch products.

Confluence's constant backdrop is mountains. The blue-tinged hillsides of the Appalachians rim the river town in a way that will make you start looking around for the Norman Rockwell signature.

"I definitely want to stay here tonight," said my wife.

"I thought you wanted to keep riding."

"Well, I changed my mind. Now we're staying."

Heavy is the head that wears the crown.

We eased into town on fumes. I was thirsty and I needed to get off my seat. Confluence is a functioning town, but you see very little evidence of modern life here. There are no billboards, no heavy traffic, no Olive Gardens, no guys on street corners dressed in togas, waving cardboard signs advertising five-dollar pizza. There are old churches, old houses, and a lot of old people. Even the supermarket was a throwback to the days when the *Brady Bunch* was still on primetime.

I walked through the Food Mart double doors, grabbed a shopping basket, and found a brochure that advertised a local guest house. It was a beautiful home with a gracious porch overlooking the rivers. I patted my pockets and suddenly realized I was phoneless. So I went to the manager's desk and asked to borrow the phone. The woman behind the desk looked at me like I had just burped in public. I suppose it is pretty bizarre in today's world to be without a phone. Even homeless people own cell phones.

"You wanna use our *phone?*"

"Yes, ma'am."

"Don't you have a cell phone?"

"No."

"Nobody ever asks to use our phone."

I jingled the change in my pockets. "Yes, well, now you can't say that anymore."

I dialed the number on the brochure. The lady who answered was beyond friendly. By the tone of her voice, I could tell that her hair was also white.

"Of *course* we have room," the woman said. "We got plenty of room tonight. You can stay in the master suite. How's that sound?"

The master suite? Heavens. I could have danced a jig. Then she told me the price, and I nearly suffered a mild infarction. It was highway robbery. We were definitely going to need more Little Debbies.

Jamie and I left the supermarket with plastic bags draped over our handlebars, circling the town looking for the house on the brochure. We cruised through the side streets and alleys and took in the town.

About eight hundred people live in Confluence, and they keep the place looking spectacular. In the epicenter of the borough is a green central park with a gazebo and several benches. Antique Queen Anne houses pepper the town. We saw people walking dogs. We saw neighbors having conversations on porches. Music drifted from an unseen window. Was it Artie Shaw or Benny Goodman? Do people still listen to this kind of music? Where were we? *When* were we?

We passed chrome-bumpered antique Chevys glittering in the dusk, whitewashed front porches crowded with wicker furniture, and flags—there must have been an American flag winging from every upright surface in town. It was nice.

I passed an old lady kneeling in her rose garden, wearing a straw sun hat. Old men clipped shrubbery with scissor-style hedge trimmers. We even rode past a postman walking the streets, wearing a satchel.

"Can you believe this place?" said my wife, pulling over at a scenic overlook nestled between two Victorian-style homes. She pointed to the Youghiogheny River in the distance, merging with two other tributaries far below us. A picturesque white home stood perched atop a soaring bluff overlooking the rivers. It almost looked too good to be true.

"Wow. Is that where we're staying?"

"Once we remortgage our house, yes."

I walked into a small restaurant surrounded by multitudes of bikes stabled for the evening. The place was overrun with cyclists in shorts tight enough to jeopardize one's procreative capacity. It was so loud inside I could hardly concentrate long enough to read the menu. Jamie was back at the boarding house, taking a shower. I was picking up dinner.

Miss Congeniality behind the counter had pink hair and multiple facial piercings, like she'd fallen into a tackle box. Her attitude was that of a pit viper.

She grabbed a pad and pen. She touched the pencil to her tongue and simply said, "Yeah?"

My, but aren't they friendly in Pennsylvania?

I glanced at the menu. "I'll take two cheeseburgers."

"We're out of burgers."

I looked around at the mass of people eating burgers and drinking glasses of amber beer. Heads back, mouths open, laughing with unchewed ground beef in their mouths.

"But other people are eating burgers."

"We just sold out."

"How about chicken tenders?"

She shouted back to the kitchen. "Hey, Sal! Any chicken tenders?"

Sal shouted back, "Not no more!"

"Out of chicken tenders," she said.

"How about the meatball sandwich?"

She shook her head. "Out."

"Bread and water?"

She just looked at me.

I closed the menu. "How about you tell me what you do have?"

"Got a grilled chicken salad."

"I'll have two of those."

"What kinda dressing?"

"As much ranch as you can give me without getting fired."

"We're outta ranch."

Give me strength.

On my long walk home, the weather was turning foul. The swirling clouds in the sky were moving aggressively over the dark mountaintops in odd patterns. The weather can change quickly in the mountains. A thousand miles south, somewhere in Alabama, Hurricane Sally was slamming into the coastline. This change in weather could already be felt all the way up in the mid-Atlantic.

When it started to pour, I darted beneath the overhang of a building with a modest steeple and tried to wait it out, but the rain was blowing horizontally. The wind picked up. The street turned into the mighty Mississippi, and I was getting saturated.

I tried the church's front doorknob. It was unlocked, so I rushed inside.

"Hello?" I said a few times, creeping into an empty vestibule. I didn't want to startle a janitor or get pepper-sprayed by a church secretary named Mildred.

I waited, but nobody answered.

"Hello? Anyone here?"

No signs of life.

I found myself exploring the halls while the rain fell harder. The place was aged, but not antique. More linoleum than wood. Shallow ceilings. All-weather carpet that was once light khaki but was now brownish green. Outdated light fixtures that constantly hummed a middle C.

I grew up in buildings like this.

Like many small-town Americans my age, I was reared in dinky Sunday school classrooms and outmoded fellowship halls, beneath the instruction of the coiffed-hair brigade. The women who raised me wore inch-thick nylons, beehive hair-dos, and Estée Lauder Youth-Dew bath powder. They taught us to say, "Yes, ma'am," and "No, ma'am," under threat of our own lives. Places like this were home away from home. What were the odds that I found myself in a chapel on the anniversary of my father's end?

I found a paper bulletin and thumbed through it.

I was getting all the warm feelings of boyhood. Bulletins in old churches all read the same. And they haven't changed much from the days when Sister Penny Lou used to print ours on the mimeograph machine, producing some of the greatest typos in history, such as: "Remember in prayer those who are sick of our community and church," and "Deacon Bryant Wallace says, 'I upped my pledge, up yours.'"

I found my way into the sanctuary. I sat in the front pew and took in the silence for a while. Head erect. Eyes open. My father would have been sixty-seven if he had still been alive. I looked at the vaulted ceilings and the crucifix over the altar.

I grew up in evangelical congregations like this one. Our buildings came complete with window-unit AC and popcorn ceilings. I learned all the lyrics to "In the Garden" and all three hundred and forty-six verses to "Just as I Am." Therefore I don't feel much attraction to modern megachurches. Don't get me wrong, I have nothing against fog machines and stage lights, but ordering a Starbucks in a church lobby just feels wrong. I grew up in a simple tradition, alongside rural folks who wore the same polyester outfit to church each week. My mother owned two church dresses. My father had two neckties; one for funerals, one for real-estate closings. Our preachers shouted. We had an organist named Wanda. We had altar calls every single week even though we never had any visitors.

I feel fortunate to have been born at the tail end of an era that had not yet embraced amplification systems. We had no drum kits behind plastic cages, no Eddie Van Halen guitars, no large screens broadcasting updated lyrics to "Amazing Grace." We had out-of-tune Mason & Hamlin pianos, tattered hymnals predating the Cold War.

I realize I am romanticizing small churches and their parishioners. It wasn't all casseroles and roses. When I was a kid, for example, my people talked about hell more often than we talked about the other place. And even in Protestant congregations, suicide victims like my father weren't exactly regarded as saints. But there were some exceptional human beings among us too. And places like this bring it all back for me.

There were the elderly women who delivered food to our house for a solid year after my father's death. Always under the cover of darkness. Old man John did all our home repairs, and although my mother tried to pay old John, the cash always mysteriously ended up in our mailbox. There was the elderly preacher at my father's funeral visitation, who walked through the receiving line with the sole mission of speaking to me. He wore a cheap suit and a determined look on his face. He didn't even attend our church. He'd simply read about my father's death in a newspaper and drove several hours to get there.

And of course, I met my wife in a church like this. We were married in a clapboard building on Matthew Boulevard. The building had a crooked steeple and water spots on the ceiling. We exchanged vows beneath those water spots.

I sat for nearly thirty minutes listening to the rain heave itself onto the roof. The noise sounded like static on the radio. I tucked my head. I closed my eyes.

I was interrupted.

"Can I help you?" said a voice from the back.

It was a woman with hair that leaned more toward blue than white. She was shuffling down the aisle. She didn't look glad to see me, but she didn't look upset either. She wore that attentive but helpful look all church ladies wear. She spoke in an old-time Yankee accent that made you certain she knew her way around a vat of potato salad.

I stood.

"I'm sorry if I startled you," she said. "It's just that I'm about to lock the doors for the night, hon."

Hon.

"Yes, ma'am. I'm sorry. I was just trying to avoid the rain."

"Oh, it's just a gully washer out there, isn't it?"

"Yes, ma'am."

She glanced at my to-go bag of food, then smiled. "My sister's son works there. They make good hamburgers."

"Not tonight they don't."

"Do you need an umbrella?"

"No, ma'am."

A crack of lightning illuminated the sky.

"Do you want a ride back to wherever you're going, hon? I have a car. I hate to send you out in this mess."

"No, ma'am, I'm just down the street."

More lightning. More thunder. The sky was really putting on a show.

She looked out the window and frowned. "Well, maybe you should wait here for a little while longer, until it lets up."

"Yes, ma'am."

She smiled again and sat beside me. I could smell Estée Lauder all over her.

"And quit calling me ma'am," she said, patting my thigh. "This is Pennsylvania, hon."

My, but aren't they friendly in Pennsylvania?

## 13

Hurricane Sally made landfall in Baldwin County, Alabama, and then moved sharply northward along the Eastern Seaboard, causing severe weather all the way up into the Carolinas and the mid-Atlantic, where sixteen tornadoes had been confirmed. And we were in the middle of it.

We had wanted to stay another night at our cozy boarding house in Confluence, but as it turns out, all bikers wanted to stay at cozy boarding houses in Confluence during thunderstorms. All the rooms in town were booked. We decided to take our chances and press on.

A heavy rain fingered its way across the rolling green landscape like a massive ghost, like it had a mind, like it was mad. White-capped runoff tumbled down hillsides. Avalanches spilled into valleys and somersaulted into rivers. The wind was so powerful it felt like we were pedaling through a cyclone. We donned our foul-weather gear and listened to the swishing sounds of our nylon sleeves rubbing against our nylon torsos. We rode for a long time until we were stymied by something blocking the trail in the distance. When we got closer, we could see that the blockage was caused by a bunch of wild turkeys, standing watch on the trail like sentinels on duty.

"Look," said my wife, cruising to a stop.

"What're we stopping for?" I hollered over the uproar of rain.

She pointed. "Turkeys."

"Wonderful. Can we keep going now?"

"Look at them."

"I'm soaked down to my undershorts."

"But they're so cute."

The turkeys' little heads moved right, then jerked left like they were having mini poultry seizures in the rain. They were hens, and I suppose they were kind of cute in an "I'm gonna peck your eyes out" way.

A gust knocked my hat off and threatened to blow me off the trail and down the mountainside. The trees looked like they were about to be uprooted. Debris was blowing across the trail.

"*Awww*," said the animal lover, dismounting. "Are the wittle bitty babies upset about the wain?"

Then the hens saw my wife and started fluttering their wings aggressively, making a lot of noise. They did not scurry away but kept sounding their battle cries. I could tell Jamie already wanted to take them home, put them in little lace dresses, and provide them with tea service.

"I wouldn't go any closer, honey," I said. "There might be a tom hanging around. Toms can be aggressive."

"I didn't know I married a turkey expert." She crept forward. "Here, turkey wurkey. Wook how cute."

I don't know why I bother.

In a few seconds nearly twenty baby poults exploded from the woods and scurried across the wet trail, waddling behind each other in a line, gobbling in bubbly voices like children at recess. They were followed by a gaggle of toms that, like I predicted, were not happy. One of the turkeys approached my wife aggressively, wings flapping. Jamie went to her bike and started fiddling through her backpack.

"What're you doing?" I asked Jamie.

"What's it look like I'm doing? The pwecious wittle birdie wirdies are hungry."

Jamie waltzed straight toward them. She squatted while the adult turkeys released some truly blood-curdling sounds.

"They look mad," I said.

"So cute . . . Here, turkey wurkey . . ."

"Especially that one. He looks like he wants to kill you."

"Mama's got a wittle Kit Kat, turkey . . ."

"Hey, I thought we were out of Kit Kats."

Once again, we see how dishonesty can chip away at the foundation of any marriage.

A few minutes later lightning rattled the night sky like the reports of rifles. The sky let loose a monsoon. For hours we chugged through the downpour. Daylight soon disappeared. Slender trees fell across the trail, and airborne foliage smacked our faces. And I am obliged, as a professional writer and longtime member of Writer's Labor Union Local Number 10, to say that it was a "dark and stormy night."

Then, somehow, Jamie and I lost each other. I guess it

was bound to happen sooner or later. One of the first things you learn on the trail is how easy it is to ride at separate tempos out there. You get so into the rhythm of your own pedaling that you quit paying attention to your surroundings. Moreover, my three wheels were much slower than Jamie's two. She could ride rings around me. But then, to be fair, she could ride rings around you too.

At first, I wasn't too concerned about being separated. We're both adults. But after a few hours of being apart, I had started to stew on the fact that we were perhaps miles apart in the vast Allegheny Mountains. I was beginning to worry.

It's eerie being in the middle of a thunderstorm by yourself in the dark woods. I had no means of communication with the outside world, no way of knowing where I was, and nobody was on the trail, there were no distant lights, no signs of life. Occasionally I called my wife's name and heard no response but the howling of the rain. She could have been eight feet ahead or eight miles ahead. There was really no way to know. I couldn't see anything through the heavy blankets of water. I couldn't hear anything but rain. Still, I kept shouting for her as the miles rolled beneath me. I didn't know what else to do.

I stopped alongside the trail to survey my surroundings. I cupped my hands beside my mouth. "Jamie! Hey!"

I saw nothing but darkness on all sides. Water shot off my hat brim in a straight stream.

This sucked.

Finally, I saw a tiny blinking red hazard light.

Hallelujah. I felt my whole body relax a little. I knew exactly where this tiny light was coming from. My wife had ordered red blinking emergency lights ($29.95) before our trip. I made fun of these lights since the idea of bicycle-hazards just seemed to scream "hall monitor!" But right now I was eternally grateful for these electric red dots, and I can't recommend them enough for other cyclists. Buy two or three. Without them I never would have known that Jamie was ahead of me in the dark. And believe me, it can get very dark out there.

Thus encouraged, I continued chasing her blinking red light for miles, keeping her flashing red dot in my immediate vision.

I had never known such discomfort, and I hope I never know it again. I had already experienced some hard rain on the trail, but nothing like this. This was the kind of rain you tell your grandkids about.

Also, my brain kept reminding me that we had paid good money to do this. Nobody was forcing us to be here. We weren't in the military. We were here of our own volition. The weather got worse. Soon I heard trees cracking in the woods and the booming sounds of falling trunks. The crashes in the forest were loud enough to make me feel as though my trike had levitated momentarily.

The effort I was expending had started to catch up with me. I was famished and weak, light-headed from hunger. I realized that I hadn't eaten anything since breakfast. My body was running dangerously low on calories, and my quadriceps were becoming wobbly. My head was a balloon, drifting several feet above my shoulders. I was ready to be finished and lying in a warm bed. Our guidebook said there was an inn ahead, but right now I would have been satisfied sleeping underneath someone's front porch.

The blinking red light ahead stopped moving.

I wondered why the light had come to a halt. Why had she quit pedaling? Maybe she had a flat tire? *No, please, God, don't let it be a flat.* The last thing I needed tonight was a flat.

I called out to the math teacher, but she couldn't hear me. So I kept moving forward until I caught up to her. Jamie was leaning on her bike with her John Deere hat cranked tightly on her head, wet strands of hair clinging to her face, a cyclone of water blowing around us.

"What're we stopping for?"

My wife pointed upward through the India-ink. "*That,*" she said bleakly, with her finger aimed above shoulder level.

I followed her gaze until I saw it. There in the obsidian night was the biggest freaking hill I have ever seen in my life.

When I was seven years old, I remember watching a man on ESPN pull a bus across a one-hundred-foot obstacle course. My uncle and cousins were in the room, watching with me. We sat slack-jawed watching Geoff Capes from the United Kingdom compete in the World's Strongest Man competition, pulling forty-four thousand pounds like a draft animal.

Geoff Capes was built like a washing machine, only with bigger thighs. He had no neck; his shoulders began just below his earlobes. His entire vascular system was visible through his crepe-paper skin, and his biceps were approximately the size of Danny DeVito.

For the "bus pull" event, Capes wore what amounted to a horse collar and towed a forty-foot MCI D-Series bus along a patch of rural highway like a team of oxen pulls a chisel plow. Beneath the massive effort, Capes's upper body was almost parallel with the pavement. His calves bulged. His face contorted like a cartoon illustration. He looked like a cerebral aneurysm waiting to happen.

That was me.

The sky was black. It was downpouring. And somewhere in the hinterlands, I was pulling a fully loaded trike uphill with a rope harness around my shoulders like a pack mule.

"You can do it!" shouted my wife between bouts of laughter. "Keep going!"

It's stunning what you learn during moments of extreme duress. I learned an indispensable lesson that night. I learned that my trike could not be pushed uphill. It could only be *pulled*. A trike is not like a bike. A bicycle can be walked uphill with no problem; just stand behind the handlebars and push. But a low-to-the-ground recumbent trike has a steering mechanism that will flop back and forth when you push the machine from the rear. You cannot reach the steering mechanism while standing behind the trike. Therefore, you cannot steer and push at the same time. If you try, your tricycle wheels do whatever they want, and the entire contraption will end up rolling downhill. And since there was no earthly way I could pedal up this vertical Everest, it was the horse collar.

My makeshift collar was fashioned by the Greatest Algebraic Mind of Our Time. She made a yoke from lengths of rope, with bungee cords to be worn around my neck. This impromptu harness was fitted to my waist and shoulders. Throughout my fitting, my wife had to excuse herself several times so that she could laugh until her gums bled. When I was sufficiently strapped to my machine like a Budweiser Clydesdale, all that was left was to channel the spirit of Geoff Capes.

Listen, I have seen the Catskills, the Adirondacks, the San Francisco Peaks, the Rockies, and the Bighorns. I have been atop Pikes Peak and gazed upon five states from 14,110 feet. I realize the Alleghenies aren't the Andes. But these were among the steepest hills I've ever walked. Furthermore, what I was doing was dangerous. One wrong step on this wet pavement and I would slip and fall, and then the weight of my trike would drag me into oncoming traffic.

Yes, traffic! I forgot to mention the traffic. To get to the inn, our trail intersected briefly with a highway that welcomed all amateur NASCAR competitors. Headlights glared. Motorists leaned on their horns. And the intermittent spray from all-season automobile tires showered us. I found myself on the shoulder of a busy throughfare, dragging a trike along the rumble strip.

When I reached the first plateau, my lungs were burning; my legs were Jell-O. I fantasized about slipping into a nice warm coma. This is when I discovered two more hills awaiting me, both steeper than the first.

By now, even the math teacher's good humor had vanished. The pain in my shoulders felt knifelike. The weight of the trike was enough to make my boots lose traction; I could hear my rubber soles sliding beneath me. I heard low-pitched moans coming from somewhere deep within my diaphragm with each striving, pitiful step. My wife trudged behind me with her bike, keeping to my rear in case I collapsed and found myself somersaulting beneath the rear axles of a Toyota Celica.

"Almost there!" my wife shouted, even though it wasn't even close to being true. We were nowhere near *there*.

"Mush!" said my wife.

## 14

*I know a* guy who spent six months hiking the Pacific Crest Trail, walking from the California-Mexico border to the Canada-Washington border. He didn't finish the whole thing, but he walked about 1,500 miles on foot, moving steadily onward, a little every day, carrying a forty-two-pound backpack. He slept outdoors for the better part of a year. He bathed in creeks and rivers. He ate dried food until his bowels turned to stone. When I asked why he did this, he had to think long and hard about his answer. You'd imagine someone who had traveled that far on foot would have been able to immediately name their reason for doing so. But he couldn't. Eventually, he just shrugged his shoulders and said without a trace of irony, "Because."

Many trail goers say something similar. On the trail, we had been asking all sorts of people why they were out there, and the most common response was a frown, followed by a few minutes of reflective thoughtfulness. During the writing of this book, I spoke to a lot of hikers and asked this question dozens of times. Nobody could ever give me a definite reason.

Here are some of the verbatim answers I received: "I dunno, sounded like fun." "Well, I figured, why not?" "Don't really know. Just kinda wanted to do it." "Beats the heck outta me."

Trails cast strange spells over their victims. I don't know what you call this magic—stupidity, maybe. But the fact is, very few travelers can tell you *why* they are out there.

Including me.

I opened my eyes, and I could smell Folgers.

I blinked at the ceiling a few times and tried to place myself in time and space. The soreness in my body was exponential. Where was I? Who was I? Why did my legs hurt? *Why?* I kept asking myself. *Why am I doing this?*

Jamie delivered hot coffee to me in bed.

"Rise and shine, mule," she said.

We were in a charming Victorian home, on the second level. Outside my window was the skyline of Rockwood. I sat upright against the headboard. I looked around our room. It was strewn with gear, bags, water, bottles, and dripping jackets. It looked like we had simply shed our supplies and fallen into bed the night before. That is, of course, exactly what we'd done.

The coffee was working miracles. I was in the pleasant daze that accompanies my first hit of caffeine. I crawled into the shower, still holding the blistering coffee mug and sipping between scrubs. I let the hot water roll over me until the inn's water heater gave up the ghost. When I emerged from the bathroom's cloud of steam, I was limping on raw legs and tender feet. I saw the math teacher fully dressed in rain gear and packing our saddlebags. I felt a sudden dread swallow me when I glanced out our bed-and-breakfast window and saw it was still raining. We had miles to go. Miles and miles.

And miles.

I collapsed on the bed, still wrapped in my towel. I was asleep within sixty seconds.

She nudged me awake. "You can't sleep."

"Just a few minutes," I groaned.

She began shaking the bed.

"Please, stop doing that," I said.

Now she was on her knees, jumping on the bed.

"Got to keep pedaling," she said. "Got to keep moving."

"Go away."

*"The wheels on the bike go round and round . . ."*

So we saddled our bikes in the morning torrent and began pedaling. Simple as that. We were moving again.

It's an interesting feeling to have the entire purpose of your life boiled down into one verb: pedal.

The math teacher was in the lead. "How ya doing back there?" she said from time to time.

I moaned.

"Sorry, didn't hear that," she'd say.

"Please don't ask me how I'm doing."

I lunged my legs against my pedals and winced with each movement. My trike had started making frightening noises again. I heard various bits of metal falling onto the ground beneath me. But I was beyond caring. Soon I was accompanied by an incessant clacking noise coming from my wheels.

The funny thing is, people expect to enjoy these trails. They expect to have a marvelous time the whole way through. People such as, for example, Jamie Dietrich. After all, why else would anyone be out here? Except it doesn't work that way—at least not unless your sense of fun is a little warped. There are good days out here, sure. But there are some really crummy days too. I think it's all about ratios.

We circled Rockwood in low gear to warm up our muscles for the morning. We cruised through the downtown of brick storefronts and shop windows that looked like a throwback to the turn of the century. Once my blood was moving again, like mud through a sippy straw, we took to the trail once more.

"You ready to go to Maryland?" said my wife.

"No."

We pedaled like it was our profession because in a way it was. We were soon surrounded by copses of trees and the deafening white noise of Hurricane Sally.

Even now, I still can't tell you why we were there.

# 15

*Just when we* didn't think the rain could get any worse, surprise, it got worse. We took shelter beneath a small bridge spanning the Eastern Continental Divide and ate a pathetic lunch while a heavy shower hammered the earth and claps of thunder shook the foundations of the Appalachian Mountains. Several other bikers were hiding beneath the bridge doing the same thing. Nobody looked happy. My wife was eating a Snickers she'd managed to keep hidden from me. I was eating—wait for it—a beef stick. We sat in silence, watching water pelt the universe. It was an unusually cold day. We were both shivering and trying to catch our breath. I've seen movies depicting the former Soviet Union that were cheerier.

"I can't feel my hands," I said.

"Quit complaining. It's not that bad."

"Maybe not when you're eating a Snickers."

She shrugged. "I'm not that cold."

"Is there another Snickers in your bag?"

"No, but we have plenty of beef sticks."

The Eastern Continental Divide, one of the six hydrographic divides in the United States, separates the Eastern Seaboard from the Gulf of Mexico watershed. The ridge stretches from Florida to Ontario. It's the highest point on the trail, standing at 2,392 feet. All water on one side falls into the Atlantic, and on the other side everything flows Gulfward. At one time in colonial America, the Appalachian Divide was considered the edge of the New World. King George III issued a proclamation stating that no settlements west of this line were allowed by colonists. This really chapped the hides of our forefathers and was a key factor leading to a revolution. This was, in a way, the land dispute that started a nation. Don't say I never taught you nothing.

The thing is, when you reach the divide, it's all downhill from there. Literally. The rest of the trail is like a ski jump. And this is something to get jazzed up about, especially when lightning is flickering above you, you are saturated down to your underbritches, and the nerve sensation in all four of your cheeks is dead. Until now, the trail had been taking us steadily uphill. But after you leave the divide, it's a downhill coast.

The rain finally let up, although not much, and the bikers beneath the bridge, including our two pale heroes, mounted their machines and tore off for parts unknown.

After the divide, you only have to ride a short distance until you arrive at another benchmark, the Big Savage Tunnel. Picture a gaping black hole in a granite mountain á la Wile E. Coyote. That's the Big Savage Tunnel, and it is a stunning sight when you first arrive—that is, if you can even see it through the layers of frog-killing rain.

My wife dismounted inside the mouth of the tunnel and read from our waterlogged information pamphlet in the same voice she used in her classroom.

"'Big Savage Mountain and its tunnel were both named after John Savage, an early surveyor who, in 1736, barely avoided becoming a victim of cannibalization when he was surveying this land in the wintertime . . .'"

"Cannibalization?" I said. "Does it really say that?"

"'. . . When the surveyor's party fell on hard times and were starving to death, John Savage offered his body up for food, but his friends declined and chose not to eat him.'"

"You're making that up."

She handed me the trifold brochure. "See for yourself."

We stood inside the monstrous mineshaft. Dozens of bicyclists were zipping in and out of the tunnel. The end of the GAP was getting closer, and there was a definite renewal of energy among our fellow cyclists. You could just tell people were excited to be near the end of the GAP.

"Well," said Jamie, "I think it was a noble gesture, to offer his body up for food. I think it was an act of heroism, chivalry."

"Would you eat me? If we were starving?"

She gave me a once-over and zeroed in on my scrawny thighs.

She frowned, then hopped onto her bike, and sped

through the tunnel, leaving me to deal with the fact that I'm unfit for a main course.

The Big Savage Tunnel was impressive. At over half a mile long, hewn through acres of granite, it has a way of making you feel very small. The underground air was even icier than the frigid air outside the tunnel. Each breath bit my lungs and made my windpipe tingle with cold. The ceiling-mounted lights streaked over us and cast a sickly pink glow onto everything. It felt like cycling through earth's GI tract.

Everyone sings in the Savage Tunnel. Nobody can fight it. That's part of the deal. The reverberations are simply too alluring for the common idiot to resist. We were soon accompanied by the echoes of spooky voices from unseen bikers who sang at the top of their lungs. I heard a version of "I Will Always Love You," "Jailhouse Rock," and a truly bloodcurdling rendition of "Popeye the Sailor Man."

The voices got louder when we reached the middle portion of the tunnel. After a few moments I decided all this singing was one of the most ridiculous displays of immaturity I'd ever witnessed in my life, and I wanted to be part of it.

I began singing. *"Ninety-nine bottles of beer on the wall . . ."*

Midsong, a bicycle pulled up beside me, and someone started singing along. I turned to see a familiar cyclist. Sandy's voice was startlingly good. She sang harmony with me.

"Glee club," said Sandy. "Three years. What about you?"

"First Baptist choir, thirty to life."

No laugh. I need better material.

"How did we manage to get so far ahead of you?" I asked. "I thought you'd be done with the trail by now."

I watched this woman with great curiosity. I noticed the mottled scar on her neck where a PICC line once was. I hadn't noticed that scar before. I also noticed several new stitches on her elbow, some bandages, and a rainbow of bruising on her thighs.

"Had a little accident," she said. "Put me behind schedule."

She showed me scrapes and bruises on her arms and legs.

"I took a spill back in Meyersdale," she said. "But, hey, I'm okay. I can still ride. Got to keep going, right?"

"The wheels on the bike go round and round."

"Right you are." She looked at me. "Good news is, we're almost done with the GAP."

Good news indeed.

With that, she bid me goodbye and sped ahead. I watched as her body extended like a warbird, midflight, speeding out of the tunnel like she'd been shot from the barrel of a .44. Her thighs were slim trunks of muscle, and her calves looked like overinflated footballs. Sandy burned past every biker on the trail with blinding velocity and still managed to give everyone the same friendly, disarming smile when she passed.

No sooner had Jamie and I exited the tunnel than we hit another major landmark and crossed the Mason-Dixon Line. The demarcation line originally surveyed by Charles Mason and Jeremiah Dixon in 1763 was marked by two stone pillars representing the boundary between two vastly different regions. On one side, the land of nasal accents and beef stroganoff. On the other side, Mama. We posed for a picture with Jamie's ginormous iPad.

I kept thinking about Sandy throughout the day. She was always on my mind. Only one year earlier, I had lost two very close friends to cancer. And as I write this book, my best friend's wife is steadily declining from the same disease. It seems like every few months, someone else within my inner circle is diagnosed with cancer.

In my life as a columnist, I have interviewed a lot of people in hospital beds. I've written dozens, maybe even hundreds, of columns about people with terminal illnesses, including children in oncology wards. I've found that most terminal patients say the same things. Nobody, without exception, has ever said they wished they were more successful. Nobody has ever told me they wish they would have owned a bigger house or that they would have worked more. People always say things like, "I wish I would've been true to myself," "I wish I would have kept in touch with old friends," "I wish I would have traveled more."

Maybe this was my *why*. Maybe being out here was our way of doing what living people do. Breathing and moving. Seeing and touching. Either way, we kept riding toward the GAP's finish line in Cumberland, and I was ready to be done.

The math teacher pulled alongside me. "Mush!" she said again before leaving me in a rooster tail of dust.

I'd about had enough of her.

My wife screeched to a stop.

"Look," she said, pointing at an itty-bitty Cumberland, Maryland, in the distance, burrowed in the greenery of the far-flung Alleghenies. "We're almost there."

And here's how it will happen.

Just when you think you're sick of this infernal trail, just when you find yourself tired of trying, tired of pedaling through the walls of rain, tired of working, tired of eating food that was packaged in plastic sometime around the construction of the Panama Canal, tired of looking for a clearing that might serve as an impromptu restroom, then suddenly you're coasting downhill.

Until now, you have been riding upward. Now it's a descending grade, and this changes everything. Momentum is carrying you. An unseen force whisks you away. Not your muscles. Not your will. But gravity. You are no longer working. You are no longer grappling. You are moving. If I were a great thinker, I would compare the trail to life itself. But I'm not a great thinker. So I will shut up.

We approached an overlook on Savage Mountain that completely stole the show. Nothing on the trail had compared to this. We pulled over. You could see for miles over the miniature treetops, which extended to the horizon. The forests of pines and maples quilted themselves over the rises and falls of a mountainous topography. We admired the panorama of patchwork farmland, knitted together, laid upon alpine terrain, dotted with little red barns, mirrored lakes, and livestock in the pastures.

This was how the trail was supposed to look. Miles below us was a miniscule city that looked like it belonged in a train model set. Church steeples cropped up from the skyline by the dozen. Cumberland was an entire city of steeples from this angle. We crawled back onto our cycles and let gravity carry us the rest of the way. My wife blitzed ahead of me. Her right arm was extended in our favorite sign language salutation. I returned salute, but she was too far ahead to notice.

Then . . .

It was all over.

Just like that, the GAP ended. Our cycles were suddenly inert. There was no more trail before us. We cruised into downtown Cumberland amid coffee shops, speeding SUVs, barbecue pits, and places serving crab cakes to hungry tourists wearing Spandex. We found ourselves parked beneath a steel banner arching over the trail. A large brass plate was embedded in the cobblestones beneath us, marking the end. We had finished the Great Allegheny Passage. Honestly, I didn't expect to feel anything when this happened. I thought this moment would come and go and be about as triumphant as opening a jar of JIF. But this was much more substantial. We had done something big. Together we stared at the mountain vista behind us, catching our breath, slurping water from bottles.

"We biked over all that," said my wife.

"And triked," I said.

"Look at those mountains."

"Look at *all* those mountains."

"Amazing."

"Yeah."

A moment like this is more profound than you're ready for. Especially when you see the reactions of others nearby. I did not expect the kind of emotion I was seeing. It's only a trail, I was thinking. But for many people, this is much more than a trail.

I saw a man embracing his teenage son. I saw two gray-haired people holding each other and crying. There was a young woman in an oversized bike helmet, kissing the cheeks of her daughter, who had been waiting at the end of the trail and holding a poster that read:

## WE LUV YOU MOM

"I can't believe we just pedaled over all *that*," said my wife.

We hobbled from our cycles onto linguini legs and threw our arms around each other. We both smelled horrible, but it was perfect.

Other cyclists were weaving around us, on both sides, skidding to victorious stops, high-fiving, and laughing. We heard various bursts of spontaneous applause from family members cheering for loved ones. We saw people slinging arms around the shoulders of total strangers. There was the cracking open of ceremonial Gatorades. I saw two college guys in soccer jerseys clapping each other's backs and speaking in a foreign language. Portuguese, I think it was. I saw a middle-aged couple FaceTiming with grandkids. I saw a young man praying.

My wife and I pressed our foreheads together. I could smell her ripe sweat as she met my gaze with her two eyes. She grabbed my face in both hands and forced her mouth over mine in a hard kiss. It was the Mount Fuji of kisses. The kind of kiss that feels a lot like a slap.

Then she drew back and said, "Yes, I would totally eat you if it came down to it."

PART 3

# The Chesapeake and Ohio Canal Towpath

*Nothing is more beautiful than the loveliness of the woods before sunrise.*

—GEORGE WASHINGTON CARVER

## 16

*A breakfast joint.* A sunny day. We were waiting for the hostess to seat us. The smell of bacon was everywhere. Overhead George Jones was singing about wrecking his pickup. The sound of a pedal steel guitar whined, and all was right with the world. My wife and I stood in the diner entrance, wearing civilian clothes. The place was swarming with cyclists in workout wear that fit tighter than sausage casing.

It was loud. Infants were screaming, mothers scolding, and waitresses barking at short-order cooks. We were definitely back in the real world. There was a pandemic still going on, one we'd almost forgotten about on the trail. But you could not forget things like global epidemics when you rejoined the human race. Newspapers never quit talking about it. TVs blared it. It was in every conversation with strangers. It was on signs around town. The world seemed like it was on the brink of chaos. And somehow, we had forgotten all about it out on the trail.

We were in great moods, fully rested, well fed. And we had new phones with facial recognition and thumbprint technology. You must have facial recognition and thumb-print technology, the phone saleswoman told us. We would be paying off our new phones until the second coming of John Wayne.

We had spent a few nights in a Cumberland hotel, living the good life. We wasted entire days wearing terry-cloth bathrobes and eating vending-machine foods. I read a crime novel from the hotel library. I took frequent naps. It is marvelous what hot showers and unlimited ESPN can do to a man. I had written a few columns about our travels that had been picked up by newspapers in Pennsylvania, Maryland, and West Virginia. It was the first time I'd been published in northern newsprint. I realize this doesn't sound like a big deal, and it's not really. But it meant that I was working again.

A few days' rest had restored our energy levels. And most importantly, it helped us come to a decision about the remainder of the trail. We had decided to quit. We would not keep going on the Chesapeake and Ohio towpath. We were in total agreement on this. The GAP had been tough on our bodies, and the rainy weather had made it downright nightmarish. I was having ridiculous back pain from a past surgery, and my wife's hands had gone numb from leaning her bodyweight on her handlebars. They call it "cyclist's palsy."

So we were finished, namely because, in Trail World, the GAP trail is akin to preschool, whereas the C&O trail is medical residency. I'm not saying we are wimps, but I'm also not saying we aren't.

During our brief layover in Cumberland, too many trail

veterans had been telling us how the towpath was in disrepair, overgrown and swampy from recent rains. Hurricane Sally had turned the entire trail into a decaying casserole of misery. Many who had attempted the C&O trail seriously advised against it. Most of these were people sitting outside our hotel, covered in dried blood and grapefruit bruises, with onion-skin layers of scrapes and gashes covering their limbs. "Don't do it," they'd say in foreboding voices. It was all the convincing I needed. Case closed. It was time to go home.

While we waited for a seat, I studied a map hanging on the wall behind me. It was a line drawing of the Chesapeake and Ohio Canal, in all its undulating glory. A cheery red line meandered across the topography like a big worm, outlining a route that followed every curve of the Potomac. I was struck with how much longer the trail looked than I remembered. This made me feel even more satisfied with our agreement to return home.

"You think we're making the right decision?" said my wife.

"Oh, absolutely." I was unflappable. "Not a doubt in my mind. This is the smart thing to do."

She traced the route with her finger. "Really? I mean, we've come this far. I mean, this map makes it look sorta . . . fun."

I cleared my throat loudly, signifying we were done here. "Supposed to be great weather today. Wonder how the Braves are doing?"

Her words were barely audible. "We'll probably never be here again."

"Amen."

There is a reason historians call the canal the "grand ditch." The canal is the granddaddy of all ditches. The towpath's two swampy wagon ruts plunge through vine-covered, daylight-squelched, dense, suffocating miles of unrelenting poison sumac. On a bicycle, it's a hard-going trail. On a tiny trike, it's suicide. We were most assuredly doing the right thing by quitting.

Still, the math teacher pressed an index finger on the Plexiglas-covered map. She followed the route all the way through, wearing a wistful look. I watched as her finger slid from Cumberland to Williamsport, then over to Martinsburg, Harpers Ferry, through miles of Maryland, toward the Pennsylvania border, through the state of West Virginia, and across the tip of Virginia. Her finger finally petered out after Washington, DC, somewhere around Georgetown. Good heavens, it was long.

My wife was half smiling. "Three whole states on one trail."

"Yep."

"Three *whole* states."

"We really dodged a bullet."

"Three."

The hostess called our name and seated us in a tattered vinyl booth with knife carvings on the table. We plopped our saddlebags and gear into the seats. Outside the nearby window were our two parked cycles, like hobbled horses on the mesa. There had been reports of recent cycle thefts in the area. I would have given someone several hundred bucks to

Sean Dietrich

confiscate my tricycle. I even would have thrown handfuls of
rice at them as they drove away.

Before the waitress approached, the math teacher was
already staring out the café window, lost in her own thoughts.
This made me uncomfortable. This is a woman who is never
quiet. I had a perfect view of her quarter-Choctaw profile in
the morning light, and her eyes were not with me; they were
out there again.

She didn't look at me when she spoke. "Why did it take
us so long to finally do this? What's held us back for so long?"

I said nothing.

"How come we never do anything big? How come all we
do is tread water and pay bills?"

I shrugged. "Life gets busy."

It sounded pathetic even to my own ears.

"Do you know all I could think about when we were out
there?" she said.

"No."

"I kept thinking about how I didn't want this to end. I
didn't wanna just go home and do laundry and go back to
life as usual. I kept telling myself, we're gonna do more things
like this, we're gonna live, you know? Keep doing memorable
things. I don't want to go out with a life half lived. I wanna
do something special."

Here we go again.

"Honey, we just did something special. Where have you
been for the last million miles? It was so special I can't even
walk without crying."

147

She reached across the table to rest her warm hand on mine. This is how wars are won.

"Don't you get it?" she said. "We're not finished." She paused for effect. "I think we should keep going."

"This is not happening."

"Listen to me."

"This is *really not* happening."

"We might never be in Cumberland again. This could be our only chance to do something great."

I gestured to the window. "Honey, I just did something great. I've been riding a Playskool tricycle all week. I deserve a medal. That thing is about to fall apart. There's no way I'm taking that busted piece of—"

We were interrupted by a waitress holding a notepad. "I'm sorry, I can come back if you're not ready."

The woman was midforties, red hair piled atop her head like a cast member from *Alice Doesn't Live Here Anymore*. She handed us a couple of menus and asked us: "So which trail are you doing? GAP or the Chesapeake?"

I started to answer but was cut off by the math whiz.

"We're considering the Chesapeake," said Jamie. "What's your opinion? Should we do it?"

I laughed, patted my wife's hand, and addressed the waitress. "You'll have to pardon my wife. She skipped her lithium today. We're not doing another trail. I'll take three eggs over medium and two strips of bacon."

Jamie kept her eyes on the waitress and waited for the woman's answer. Nobody paid attention to me.

The waitress twisted her mouth then said, "Well, last week my brother did the C&O. He said it's really soupy. Pretty bad out there. Lotta snakes."

"Snakes," I said.

"It's a national park," said Jamie, looking at me. "How bad can it be?"

The waitress glanced out the window and narrowed her eyes into hardened little slits. "Oh, it can get real bad, all the rain we just had. My brother said he'd never seen the trail in such horrible shape. Said it was mud up to his ankles sometimes."

"Yes, but did he finish the trail?" asked my wife.

"Oh sure, he finished, but he's an outdoorsman, you know? He loves all that rugged stuff. Setting bones and whatnot."

"But did he *enjoy* the trail?" I said. "That's the bigger question."

The waitress had to think about this. "Well, I guess he did. But he was stuck out there for a few days. Helped rescue a dad and his son who almost died out there. Had to carry their bikes several miles through mud. Had to climb over fallen trees, stuff like that. But I guess it's doable. Breakfast specials are on the back. Let me know when you're ready."

I enunciated slowly. "*Carried* their bikes."

"Doable," said my wife.

It would be the last time anyone saw us alive.

## 17

*In 1954* they were going to turn these woods into an interstate. It's hard to believe, but it's true. The proposals on Capitol Hill were to mow down the historic C&O Canal lands and create an asphalt parkway. The *Washington Post* published an editorial in full support of the project. The freeway was as good as built.

Enter Supreme Court Justice William O. Douglas. Douglas, a stern-faced Scot who looked more like a Presbyterian vacuum salesman than a judge, was an avid hiker and outdoorsman. He publicly opposed the parkway by challenging a group of newspapermen to join him in walking the towpath so they could see the land for themselves. They agreed. Douglas set out on an eight-day hike with fifty-eight enthusiastic journalists—most of whom wore the wrong kinds of shoes. Douglas's companions couldn't keep up, and after a few miles, they started dropping like English majors. The terrain was too unforgiving. By the end of the 184.5-mile trail walk, Douglas only had nine left in his party.

But the scheme worked. The *Post* changed its tune and

rallied to protect the canal lands. Soon the C&O's towpath was being cleared for hiking, and a bicycle trail was built by dumping bluestone over the same muddy wagon ruts George Washington had once trod.

But the canal lands weren't fully protected yet. Nothing guaranteed that this land wouldn't be plowed down and turned into another I-95. That is, until Congressman DeWitt S. Hyde of Maryland championed the idea by introducing a bill to create the Chesapeake and Ohio Canal National Historical Park.

Hyde believed that the canal was "a poor man's national park." He believed that American families in the mid-Atlantic should have a national park that was on par with the Rockies or Yosemite, and he claimed this park was already in their own backyard. "This park," Hyde said, "will run through probably one of the most beautiful least known and least developed river valleys in the east."

His bill got some attention. And because this is America we're talking about, a great nation with a reputation for conservation, with deep respect for our natural monuments, a country that *invented* national parks, absolutely nothing happened. In fact, Congress laughed at Hyde so hard they nearly dropped their golf clubs.

Nobody important would pay attention to Hyde's bill until January of 1961. And even then, salvation came only days before Eisenhower left the White House, when, in a fleeting moment of goodwill, the president proclaimed the canal property a national monument. After that, it took five more years for Congress to quit flinging paper footballs at each other during joint sessions and turn the canal lands into an actual park.

Thus, fifteen years and three presidential administrations after Douglas's first hike with a bunch of journalists, the Chesapeake and Ohio National Historic Park finally became a reality in 1970. It was a miracle the park ever happened at all.

I bring all this up for a very important reason. Word count, baby.

But also because the arresting beauty of the canal lands will stop your heart and make your knees shaky. Congressman Hyde was right. This national park is every bit as beautiful as Yosemite. The idea that this place was going to be turned into a highway would be like tearing down Yellowstone to build a Big Lots.

My wife and I spent our first day cycling the canal in solitude, lost among silver maples, paw paws, and American sycamores at every bend. We followed a winding path that clung to a meandrous river. We paused beside the quiet canal, frosted with lime-green moss, lit with dappled sunlight, and it was all so perfect it might as well have been a mirage. We saw storybook trees, golden hayfields, distant farmhouses, and the antique hermitages of lock operators, who lived on-site and looked after the canal locks three centuries ago. There were thick canopies of oaks, shading our path like umbrellas, and aqueducts made of hand-hewn stone from the days when teenagers were signing up to fight Revolutionary wars.

It's not hard to see why George Washington adored this land. This canal was his magnum opus. He gave his life to seeing it built and oversaw every mile of its construction. He died two years before the canal's completion. That is why, at times on this secluded path, I half expected to happen upon a ponytailed guy in riding pants carrying a Brown Bess flint-lock musket and a pheasant, taking in the serene views. And this trail was more than serene. Compared to the beauty of the C&O, the GAP trail had looked like Detroit.

The terrain, however, was a nightmare.

Back in Cumberland, people had warned us that parts of the trail were almost unpassable since the pandemic put an end to routine trail maintenance. We ignored these people, primarily because we are stupid. If anything, they were putting it mildly. We pedaled over the most uneven and slushy trail in existence. We crossed miles of bogs with chest-high grass and enormous dead trees blocking the path. There were sharp rocks, dangling vines, animal carcasses, and puddles three feet deep. At times I couldn't even see the trail; all I saw was a lake of mud and rocks. I wasn't sure my trike would survive the beating for 184.5 miles of anguish. Within a few minutes of riding, I realized I had made a grand mistake.

There was also an eerie feeling in the canal woods. We were alone out there. After several hours of slopping through the mire, boulders, and exposed roots, I suddenly realized we hadn't passed another person for upwards of eight hours. Whereas the GAP occasionally felt inhabited, and sometimes even lively, the C&O was a ghost trail. Our only company was the Potomac and the canal. Maybe a few turtles.

We spent the entire day moving slowly onward to our first campsite on the map. The weeds made it a dense jungle. Mud caked onto our bike gears like hard clay. It was as though I were riding my trike along train tracks covered in peanut butter. And bonus: our campsite was nowhere to be seen.

"Do you see the camping area?" I called to my wife.

"No. Do you?"

"Honey, I'm riding about five feet below you. All I can see is your butt."

"You should count your blessings then."

Then it started to get dark. We were still looking for our campsite, but there were no signs, no arrows, no outhouses. Nothing but tightly packed walls of grass and vines. And still it got darker. On the GAP, I thought I had experienced true darkness. That was nothing. This was impenetrable black. This was indelible ink.

When we pulled over at what we assumed was our primitive campsite, it was so murky you couldn't see your own shoes. I strapped on an LED headlamp and looked around at the thicket surrounding me. The barriers of overgrowth were armpit-high in some places. I was now becoming hyperaware of snakes.

"I think we should just keep riding," I said. "This doesn't look like somewhere I wanna sleep. I can't believe they call this a campsite."

"Keep riding? I'm tired."

"I am not sleeping here."

"You want to keep going in the *dark?*"

I glanced down the Legend of Sleepy Hollow trail. It was a great void. An abyss. Still, I would have rather taken my chances with the dark unknown trail than with the cold-blooded reptiles. "I think I'd feel more comfortable staying somewhere less . . . snakey," I said.

She vetoed this. My opinions did not exist in the vacuum of her absolute executive power. This is a woman originally from south Alabama who has childhood photographs of herself clutching snakes by the heads and smiling at the camera. She was already setting up our camp stove.

"Less talk, more action," she said. "Set up the tent."

In a few moments I was fumbling with our tent stakes, trying to keep my eye out for poison oak. The crickets were screaming, and we heard howls in the distance. Real howls. Not televised ones. You hear canine howls all the time on TV. Believe me, the boob tube doesn't do them justice.

It had been a long time since I had really roughed it. In fact, I don't know if I've ever roughed it quite like this. Then my headlamp hit a pair of reflective amber orbs in the woods. Two eyes glared back at me for a brief moment before they romped off toward the Potomac with a heavy whoosh in the underbrush.

"We've got company," I said.

My wife was now boiling water, playing Angry Birds 2. She couldn't even hear me.

"Honey, I see eyes out there," I said.

But she was too lost in the opiate glow of her phone.

The world is a food chain. And you are part of it. You can ignore this fact. You can pretend all you want that it's not real. You can buy free-range chicken breasts in sanitary plastic packages if that makes you feel like the superior species. But the truth is, you are made of meat, and the forest is one big country buffet. You rank somewhere between the salad bar and the soft-serve machine.

After the tent was erected, I heard something else move in the woods behind me. It was a loud, high-pitched rattling sound. The sound was not snakelike, but more like a giant cricket. The maraca rattled again, and I wanted to get on my trike and head for Canada.

Even my wife looked up from her phone. "What was that sound?"

"I don't know."

"It was loud."

"That's what I've been trying to tell you."

She shrugged and turned up the volume on her game. "Probably just a cicada."

"If that's a cicada, it just escaped from a research laboratory."

"Just move the tent if it bothers you."

"Good idea. How about we move it to Nebraska?"

I relocated our shelter to a new place. It took some doing, but I finally repositioned us onto a new more suitable patch of poison ivy and managed to puncture two impressive holes in the fabric throughout the process. Our tent was now about as watertight as cheesecloth.

Then my wife shrieked. "Hey, I think something just moved past my feet."

"What?"

"A snake. I see a snake."

"Quit screwing around."

"No, I mean it. It's a snake. Look."

She was telling the truth. Only it wasn't just *a* snake. It was two snakes. These two amorous snakes were engaged in copulation in the grass near our tent. Their shiny black bodies writhed like visions from the Lake of Fire. I have never seen anything more frightening that didn't involve the Kardashians.

Throughout the night, the sounds of the forest got louder. We heard screeching, cawing, buzzing, brushing, stirring, groaning, and howling, and the rattling was getting stronger. I never fully drifted off to sleep. Not even close.

At three in the morning, my eyes blinked open when I heard footsteps plodding through our campsite. They were heavy steps, moving through the brush with a careful cadence. My breath went cold and all my sphincters tightened.

Something was out there.

My first thought was that the steps sounded human. The rhythm was manlike. I kept thinking it was some deranged cyclist or a vagrant who was going to turn us into a head-line. I placed my ear against the fabric and listened to the rustling outside our protective nylon and felt as though I were going to puke. Mark Twain once said that nothing so wonderfully focuses the mind like the prospect of getting killed. He must've camped here.

The footsteps stopped.

The footsteps started again.

Then stopped.

It was madness. I reached into my backpack and looked for something, anything, to use as a weapon but came up with little more than a phone charger. We were sitting there like lamb kabobs.

Then something leaned against our tent and our whole world tilted sideways. Judging by the indention in the tent wall, it was a snout. And judging from the size of the snout-bulge, the creature was roughly the size of a rural school district.

I tapped Jamie's shoulder and whispered, "Honey, wake up."

She did not open her eyes. She only flung my hand away. "Quit it, butthead."

"Honey . . . something's out there."

"Shut up. I'm asleep."

Finally, I located my Case XX pocketknife in my backpack. I unfolded the blade and held the knife so tightly I could feel indentations forming on my palm. My knife looked more fitting for a weekend in wine country than it did as an instrument of defense. I sat awake for hours in the stillness, listening to steps move around our campsite, accompanied by the noises of heavy breathing and what sounded like crinkling paper outside. I heard mild panting, lower-pitched than a canine.

Eventually, the sounds outside faded, but I never did. I eventually fell into a very light sleep with the knife still in my hands. When morning came, my eyes snapped open. I did a physical body check to make sure I still had all my limbs and digits. I exited our tent to see our campsite scattered with bits of aluminum foil and the remnants of a bygone Lay's potato chip bag. Whatever had been out there the night before had evidently found some trail litter and licked every nanoparticle of grease from it.

I was preparing the coffee when Cinderella emerged from our tent with a blanket over her shoulders. She looked well rested.

"I can't believe you slept through last night," I said.

"Slept through what?"

"Um, Sasquatch?"

She gave me a look.

"You didn't hear it?" I said.

"Guess not."

"There was something out here." I pointed to the silver ticker tape parade around us.

"There was?"

"Yes, something hungry. Something huge. I tried to wake you up. You called me a butthead."

She blew on her coffee. "If the shoe fits."

"I'm not camping out here again."

"Oh, come on."

"I mean it. I am not doing this again."

"What, because of a few snakes?"

"No, because of *Harry and the Hendersons*."

"You're overreacting."

My mind was made up.

We packed our gear in relative silence. I'm not sure why I was so upset with her; she hadn't done anything wrong. Even so, I learned long ago that married men's brains don't think logically. We mounted our cycles. We rode into the poorly maintained woods of the Old Line State, plunging through the wilderness toward the Mountain State. I'll freely admit it: I was in a foul mood. I did not want to be here anymore. If you ask me, they should have turned this whole place into an interstate.

## 18

*The math teacher* cheered loudly when she saw the sign.

"West Virginia," she howled.

"Yay," I said flatly.

We had accumulated our third state.

A semitruck passed on my left. Another vehicle sped by my trike with an aftercurrent so powerful I lost control of my steering. The gust blew off my hat and sent it somersaulting along the highway. The semi was followed by a flatbed towing a Bobcat. Then a motorcade of diesel vehicles. My hat fluttered between lanes of traffic, miraculously unharmed.

I danced across the highway to retrieve the hat, bouncing between oncoming cars, and I kept wondering if this was how I would die. I'd survived spiders, poison ivy, mating snakes, and whatever that thing was last night, only to be killed by a speeding Peterbilt driven by a guy listening to the Judds.

I lodged my hat onto my head and jogged back to my trike. We entered downtown Paw Paw single file.

The hamlet of Paw Paw, West Virginia, is home to 508

residents and several dozen cows. The town is merely a wide spot on a two-lane highway, just off the C&O trail. The two city-limit signs are probably nailed to the same post. To get to Paw Paw from the C&O, you must leave the trail and follow a stretch of busy highway that lopes across Highway 51, thereby taking your life into your own hands. But it's worth it if you don't want to sleep with coyotes and the love-stricken legless reptiles. We rode the arcing highway bridge and were greeted by a filling station, a Dollar General, a stray dog, and that was about it. The booming metropolis had one restaurant, but it was closed because—really—the deep fryer was out of order. Farmhouses stood in the distance, and we saw a few more auxiliary cows. This wasn't the edge of the world, but you could see it from here.

Jamie had used her newly acquired smartphone to book our lodging for the evening. Our night's accommodations were—I am not exaggerating—an abandoned bus parked in a livestock pasture. I stared at our dilapidated bus with dry-rotted tires, a makeshift plywood door, and weeds growing beneath it.

"This is it?" I said.

The math teacher dismounted. "At least it's not camping."

"But it's a bus."

"Yes."

"We're sleeping in an abandoned bus?"

"Well, excuse me. Next time I'll look for a Hampton Inn and Suites."

The antiquated passenger vehicle sat with its bumper against the woods, cattle flanking the fenders on each side.

The old vehicle looked as though it had been salvaged from a junkyard. But when we opened the front door, we were greeted with a renovated vehicle outfitted with curtains, a queen bed, and an AC that could freeze the nuts off a pecan tree. I was overjoyed.

Jamie dropped her saddlebags. "Hey, not bad. And look, all the mousetraps all look brand new."

The bus turned out to be perfect. The inside was clean. The bed was comfortable. Outside were outbuildings made of unfinished wood, housing restrooms, showers, and laundry facilities. After my hot shower, I wheeled my trike into the bathroom stall and hosed the mud from my pitiful tires. The damage was worse than I'd thought. The rough ride on the C&O had taken its toll. Badly. All three tires were worn to the canvas, with threads dangling from the rims. The spokes were loose. The derailleur was hanging on the frame like a half-amputated limb.

I built a small campfire in the firepit outside the bus and tried to forget that we had more than 150 miles left to go before we hit Virginia, a distance longer than the width of Maryland. We sat staring into the flickering orange firelight in a collective daze as our bellies started to make digestive noises. These were the only noises our exhausted bodies were capable of making; nobody felt like talking.

A stray dog wandered into our campsite and sat beside me, looking for handouts.

The math teacher finally broke the silence. "I don't feel like cooking."

"Me neither."

"And I ate the last Kit Kat a few hours ago," she said.

It was a bad night.

I looked at the small rural village in the far-off. Paw Paw looked like a cluster of little lightning bugs in the night. "I'll hoof into town and see about getting some dinner."

"You really think you'll find any food?"

"These people have to eat." I stood.

The dog stood with me.

"Well, before you leave," said my wife, "can I borrow your pocketknife in case the yeti comes back?"

You have to worry about this woman sometimes.

The hike to the convenience store was about half a mile. The dog and I walked on a gravel road beneath rock-salt stars and a sky that seemed to go on forever. I passed a cow that stood beside a wire fence to watch me pass. Her big curious eyes were like eight balls. I stopped to speak to her because I was raised around cows. The old girl said nothing, but her tail flicked twice. I was hoping she'd moo at me, but no luck.

When I reached the heart of the town, I walked into the Liberty filling station, and a bell on the door dinged above me. No sooner had I entered the establishment than I realized this was a place where I could do business. It was your quintessential small-town gas-station convenience store and eatery. I also realized that we truly had crossed the Mason-Dixon Line. Not just physically, but spiritually.

I was greeted by twin fiddles playing overhead and Ernest Tubb's voice. The smells of saturated fat filled the air. A gal behind the counter called me "sweetie" and "baby" although I am neither. I half expected to see my cousin Ed Lee holding a bottle of RC and eating a Moon Pie. These were my people. I was home.

Southerners get a bad rap in today's world. The media usually gets us wrong, but that's only because they don't know us. Most people in other regions have only seen one small cross-section of our people. Thus, they don't know who we are. They know only our faults. They don't know of our devotion to family and community. They don't know of the unswerving hospitality to strangers. I'm not blaming the media exclusively. But many of these media persons have never even watched a Winston Cup Series race, if you can imagine. I think the main problem is that many newspersons depict the South as a land full of nothing but rednecks, toothless hicks, good ole boys, and religious fanatics, which isn't fair. We also have SEC football.

The middle-aged cashier looked at me from behind a deli-counter sneeze guard and placed a fist on her hip. She must have noticed the hunger in my eyes.

"You look lost, sweetie."

And I felt myself saying something along the lines of, "Feed me, please."

She grinned and got right to business. Her only question was, "How many of you are there?"

I held up three fingers. Two fingers for me.

She nodded. "Fries?"

"Oh yes, ma'am."

She then disappeared into the kitchen area.

I have heard that upscale French restaurants never ask customers what they want to eat. A true *chef de cuisine* decides what you will eat, for the chef knows the strengths of his or her repertoire; the chef knows all. She cranked up the fryer and the grill. She tied an apron around her waist and commenced to filling the gas station with the greasiest smells known to the human race.

I wandered to the back cooler to secure a Coca-Cola. Near the front window I saw an older man seated in a small booth, gazing out the plate glass in silence eating supper from a foam box.

I slid into the seat opposite him. "I guess they let papists in here," I said.

The old priest turned to me. "Saw you come in. Wondered if you were gonna pretend you didn't know me."

"Does that happen to you often?"

"When you listen to confessions for a living, yes."

"Where's your partner?"

He jerked a thumb. "He's across the street at the Dollar General, getting his dinner. He won't eat greasy stuff. Vegetarian. He'll outlive us all. But what a miserable life."

"Dinner from a Dollar General?"

He shrugged. "This is the South, ain't it?"

We get no respect.

The padre shoved a few fries into his mouth and read from a newspaper. He looked more tired than I did. I could only imagine with the treacherous miles they'd been covering on foot.

"So," he said, "how's your toy holding up?"

"Well, the trail has ruined my tires. My derailleur is holding on by a wire. I don't know how much farther I'll make it. But otherwise, it's doing great."

He shook his head. "I'm sorry."

"Me, too."

"Everyone keeps telling us it's about to get a lot worse the farther you go. We walked through miles of weeds yesterday that were up to our waists. Tell you the truth, I don't know if we can finish this."

I nodded. He was singing my song. I glanced behind me to check the status of my food. The woman behind the counter was placing slices of cheese onto hissing beef patties. I saw haystacks of fries placed into to-go boxes with pencils of steam rising from their mounds.

"You see that sky out there tonight?" the padre asked.

"Yeah."

"I've never seen a sky like that," he said.

Reba began singing overhead about the fateful night the lights went out in Georgia. This was followed by Elvis, singing about a hardheaded woman. The smells of my burger were beginning to materialize into palpable fantasies.

"Can I ask you a question, Padre?"

I didn't know how to phrase this, so I just came out and said it. "Do you believe that people who commit suicide go to hell?"

His eyebrows arched, but he was unfazed, although the mood in the room changed a little.

He said nothing at first, like all good clerics. Then he folded his paper and said, "May I ask why you're asking me this?"

"My father killed himself. Long time ago."

"Ah."

There is something cleansing about talking to strangers. Especially strangers who are professional confessors. I wasn't sure where all this was coming from.

"After he died," I said, "my father's Catholic family said he'd gone to hell."

He nodded like he'd seen it all before. And he probably had.

"Family," he grunted.

"On the day of my father's funeral, my father's family all sat on one side of the church and kept their distance from me and my sister. They didn't even speak to my mother. They wrote my sister and I out of the will. I never knew my grandparents. It was like my father had put a curse on our whole family. I guess I want to know if that's what you people believe?"

"You people."

The man ran a hand through his thin hair. He kept his eyes on the window. I should have been sorry I'd asked such a difficult question, but the beauty of talking to strangers is that there's a lot of leeway.

He heaved a sigh. "I wanna get something straight first. Are you asking if *I* believe suicide victims go to hell or if *Catholics* believe they go to hell?"

"Yes."

He faintly smiled. "Fair enough." I could see in his eyes that he was choosing his words like a guy playing a crossword puzzle. "Okay, here's what I think, and remember, what I think don't really matter, you see. Because I am just a man, in case you couldn't tell."

I nodded.

"See, I meet a lot of people who are searching for answers in my line of work. I meet them every day. And sometimes that's all religion is for folks. A bunch of answers. An endless search for more answers. Answers become the ultimate obsession. Pretty soon, you've got various groups of people claiming they found the answers, and anyone else who has *other* answers should either be beheaded or, at the very least, flayed alive."

I nodded again.

"So people start worshiping the answers. People think having answers will make them less afraid. People think that once they find these answers, there won't be no more questions. But it don't work that way. At my age, I'm learning life ain't about finding answers. It's about finding God.

"So sure, I can give you a formal answer, but in the end I'm not the one who has the final say. And if you ask me, I don't think you need an answer anyway; all anyone in this world needs is . . ."

He pointed upward.

To be honest, it was a good response with a nice little ribbon tied around it. But frankly, it was the kind of spiritual doublespeak I expected from a priest. I'm not being judgmental, but many spiritual people avoid head-on questions by simply asking more questions and being vague. They talk around the issue. Tonight, I wanted more.

"But I'm asking you what do *you* believe," I said. "Is my father in hell?"

He took a sip and shifted in his seat. He let a few moments go by.

"If I ascend into heaven," he said, "thou art there. And if I maketh my bed in hell, behold, thou art there. Psalm 139, verse eight."

Then he placed two fingers on the table to underline his point. "God doesn't *send* people to hell. He goes there with them, lays right down beside them, and he brings them through it. The psalmist wrote that. And I believe it."

## 19

*The next morning* we loaded our packs onto our bikes. I cannot ever recall being so sore as I was this morning. The hard miles from the day before were felt within each of my brittle tendons. The quiet, cool rural sunrise was accompanied by the rich scent of fresh-cut alfalfa hay and the distant bellow of livestock. The air was loud with complaining crickets. The stray dog was asleep beside our fire pit, curled in a ball. I had tried to warn him not to eat so many French fries the night before, but there are some lessons a guy must learn for himself.

I readied my trike. The machine looked like it had gone through a major land war. It sat lopsided, begging me for mercy.

My wife buckled her helmet and clapped her fingerless-gloved hands with a muffled thud. "We ready to go?"

I muttered something beneath my breath.

We started our day by following an empty highway back to the familiar trail. Soon we were back on the path to nowhere, heading for Little Orleans, Maryland. Oddly, the trail was beginning to feel like home to me. A very dysfunctional home, but home nonetheless. After enough time out here, your body adjusts to the green space. This landscape is all you have seen for days, rarely interrupted by the cold concrete of the real world. Eventually, you become part of the scenery.

After a few minutes on the trail, we were met with another mountain tunnel in the distance.

I stepped off my trike to investigate. I peered into a tunnel that shot straight through the mountain. The darkness was enveloping. There were no lights in this tunnel. Only blackness. Before me was over half a mile of lightless catwalk with a guardrail built from flimsy, dry-rotted two-by-fours. There was a pinprick of daylight at the other end. I heard gentle water running. I heard people's voices in the tunnel and the ticking of bike gears. The voices grew louder. Immediately, two LED headlamps were speeding toward me.

"Outta the way!" one voice shouted.

"Move!" said another voice.

I jogged out of the tunnel. Two young men on racing bikes clipped me and nearly knocked me off the catwalk into the canal water.

"Watch where you're going!" one cyclist shouted as he careened past, adding a few cusswords.

Jamie clicked on her headlamp and went inside first. I followed. In the dim glow of our headlamps, we could see the gangplank through the tunnel was impossibly narrow, with a steep drop-off on one side and a brick wall on the other. The footbridge was barely wide enough to accommodate someone who was walking behind their bike, let alone a dork with a trike. We inched through the tunnel slowly. My wife pushed her bike, chain clacking within the acoustics of the tunnel. I was using the horse collar.

The Paw Paw Tunnel is, hands down, the most notable feature on the Chesapeake and Ohio towpath, and this is not an opinion. It's an engineering marvel. Over six million bricks line the 3,118-foot tunnel. I'm certain this is nothing short of an astonishing visual. But I didn't see it because it was too dark inside. Someone told us there are alligators in the canal tunnel. I didn't noticed any alligators, but I heard the squeaking of rats.

"Do you think this tunnel's really haunted?" echoed my wife's voice.

"Haunted?"

"That's what the guidebook says."

"Shut up."

"I'm serious."

The tunnel has a long and sordid history. Construction began in 1836. A Methodist minister, Lee Montgomery, oversaw the project. Montgomery's Irish workers weren't skilled enough to build such a complicated tunnel, so he hired British, Dutch, and German craftsmen to help. It was a disaster. Ethnic tensions ran so high that riots broke out between immigrant workers, who started a small-scale battle among themselves and with the locals. They set fire to nearby shanties and taverns and burned down the home of a canal lockkeeper. Local legend holds that the spirit of the undead lockkeeper inhabits the Paw Paw Tunnel and whispers warnings to bikers as they pass by.

To be fair, on our long walk through the tunnel, I actually did hear a voice whispering in the darkness.

"Watch out for Sasquatch," said the whisper.

Then my wife almost peed herself.

The woods are a peculiar place. For some reason, it always seems like you're lost, even when you are not, like being lost in clouds or in your own memories. It's bewildering. It's as though you're a ladybug wandering through crowds of legs at a shopping mall. You never get a sense of where you are. There's just too much going on. Too many trees. Too many birds. Too much foliage. Too many miles ahead of you that need to be covered. Pedal, pedal, pedal. This is what you exist to do now. It doesn't matter whether you hurt or whether your thighs are seizing. Just keep pedaling. It's your job. That's the central meaning of your life now. All you can do is pedal.

Your only commodity out here is calories. So you ration them by trying to save your energy. Talking takes calories. Thinking takes calories. Breathing takes calories. You do not have calories to spare. So you don't think. You quit thinking. And you quit talking too. The only exception to this is when you find you must speak or else your wife will ride away without you. So you say in a forced whisper, "Stop, I have to pee."

Ah, yes, potty breaks. I don't mean to be overly personal, like I was raised in a barnyard, but potty breaks are an important part of trail life. If you were raised as a self-conscious evangelical, going to the bathroom outdoors can be a complicated ordeal here in the bush. You were taught not to be impolite. You come from meek rural fundamentalists who were modest people and never missed a Billy Graham Crusade telecast. You come from people who were not even allowed to put paprika on their deviled eggs because it was too showy. But everyone pees. Them's the facts.

So bathroom stops become a covert operation. The irony is that finding privacy on a trail becomes impossible. Even though these woods have been vacant all morning, Murphy's Law dictates that whenever you pull over to pee, a Boy Scout troop appears.

So your wife stands guard on the trail while you jog down a footpath searching for seclusion. When you've selected your perfect location, you assume the stance, checking both directions. Engines ready? Okay. Begin hydration evacuation sequence in five . . . four . . . three . . . two . . .

But you can't seem to make anything happen because this feels indecent. It goes against your raising. Billy Graham would never pee in the woods. But then, as if by divine grace, the river of life begins, and your bladder is feeling better.

Almost as if on cue, you hear voices. The sound of people walking through undergrowth. The sounds are getting closer. The voices are now only feet away. These are sweet, grandmotherly voices. The voices of women who bake cookies and have embroidery framed upon their walls. You can now see these people through the foliage. You see their white hair. You see their wrinkled skin. You think to yourself, *No. Please, Lord, no.*

Yes. Oh yes.

Three elderly women are on a nature walk. They are wearing sun visors, with little map pouches dangling around their necks, and sweatshirts that read something like "Kiss Me, I'm Methodist." Grannies in Reeboks, out for a stroll to identify rare species of birds. Sweet, godly women who are about to have a free viewing.

Meanwhile, there you stand. You are on this side of a trail, unable to wrap up the important business at hand. There is nothing you can do because you are male. It takes you a long time to get started in situations of anxiety. But once the water-pressure-release sequence has begun, there is no aborting without major damage to the urinary system.

So you close your eyes and pray that God will make you invisible the same way he held the sun still for Joshua, the same way he aided Gideon.

But the nightmare comes true. Three sweet old ladies pass by your half bare backside and you want to die. But to your surprise, the old ladies are incredibly polite. They hike past your haunches, less than six inches from your perpetual whiteness, and they don't show a hint of shame. Instead, they offer you a greeting. "How are ya t'day?"

You hear yourself say in return. "Oh, pretty good."

It sounds like your own words have come from another galaxy.

Then you say, "I'm really sorry about this, ladies."

One woman cackles and says, "Honey, I got six boys."

Another one says, "You ain't got nothing I ain't wiped before."

"Yes, ma'am."

When you're finished, your cheeks are hot. You sulk back to your bike, shamefaced, and your math teacher notices something is wrong. "Why are you so red?"

"There were three . . ." You can hardly bring yourself to say it. "Three old women on the trail."

"What? You mean while you were . . ."

"Yes. Now can we get outta here before they come back?"

She's laughing now. "You mean they saw your . . . ?"

You leap on your cycle. "I'm leaving now," you say.

"Did they stuff any ones or fives into your waistband?"

You ignore her. All you can do is pedal.

# 20

According to my wristwatch it was 7:04 a.m. The sun had just risen in Hancock, Maryland, and the colors of daylight were flinging their glory onto the world. And we were already on our cycles, bike saddles wedged firmly between our hindparts. Our bed-and-breakfast from the previous evening had been an old brick home located downtown. The food was decent. The beds were firm. The only downside was that we had shared the inn with a group of rowdy teenagers. Deep into the night hours, the teens held what amounted to a laughing contest in the hallway outside our bedroom walls. Then they played a few rounds of Let's Slam the Doors.

We left the bed-and-breakfast early and pulled over at the Hancock Visitor Center to eat a paltry breakfast of granola bars, which was a big improvement over beef sticks. We sat on the porch of an eighteenth-century brick home, nestled among the tulip poplars and box elders at mile marker 123 on the towpath, sipping from a thermos of coffee and trying to will our central nervous systems to start working after a mostly sleepless night.

The vibrant, plush grass spilled over into the canal water. The squirrels were playing tag in the trees. It felt like picnicking in the English countryside. One of the visitor center people told us that this land once belonged to Lord Baltimore of England in the 1700s. Whoever he was, he had great taste in real estate.

This was supposed to be our longest mileage day on the trail. We were trying to make it to Harpers Ferry before dark. It was a fool's goal.

My trike was about to fall apart. After only a few days, the C&O towpath had proven to be destructive to my cheap contraption. The man in Pittsburgh had been right. I would never make it. My tires were about to fall apart, and many of the gears had quit working. My trike wasn't the only thing suffering either. My whole body hurt from the bumps and jolts that continually threatened to throw me into the Potomac. It was a wonder that both my trike and I had made it this far without breaking down.

The visitor center was infested with bikers, all eating breakfast near the water, taking in the environs. The front porch of the center was swarming with taut bodies clad in cycling attire, eating healthful foods comprised entirely of wheat fiber, whole grains, pomegranate seeds, and organic stevia. I doubt these people even use toilets; they probably just carry little whisk brooms.

After breakfast, I began massaging my lower back with one hand, paying special attention to the six-inch scar where a neurosurgeon once cut me open after a car accident.

A few feet away, just off the trail, was an elderly couple, taking in the morning sunshine. Their bikes were weighted with a tonnage of gear. Each cycle had custom chest-high handlebars, mud flaps, and headlamps. These were no amateurs. The old man was reading a paperback while his wife, at least I assumed it was his wife, did yoga on the grass. He noticed me staring at the older woman in genuine amazement. Yoga has always impressed me. Probably because I can't do it.

The man chuckled when he saw me staring. "You think that's something, you oughta see her lick her elbow."

The woman flung a hand at him. "George, please."

"Well, it's true. She can do it."

"Honestly, George."

I smiled.

There is nothing like a morning spent among fitness enthusiasts to make you feel like a fluffy human biscuit. I looked around and saw muscular people everywhere. Most bikers were wearing tight shorts and team jerseys covered in corporate sponsorship logos even though nobody pays them to ride their bikes. Usually, their bikes were state-of-the-art, lightweight, space-age machines so advanced they didn't even need anyone to ride them.

On the GAP trail, we had seen hordes of electric bikes with full coolers strapped to their bike racks, piloted by people with koozies in their hands. But you don't see this sort of thing on the C&O. Out here, you see Hans and Franz riding carbon-fiber Cannondales.

The old man was on the last pages of his paperback. "You don't believe me?"

"Sir?" I said.

"You don't think my wife can lick her elbow?"

"Well, I've never seen it done," I said.

"Five bucks says she can do it."

His paperback was Agatha Christie's *Death on the Nile*.

"C'mon, kid. Five bucks."

"Okay," I said. "Five bucks."

"Show him, Marge."

The woman, like a vaudeville performer, stood with a shoulder-width stance, then presented her elbow to her two-person audience. Then, in a series of impossible bends and twists, the old woman strained to touch the tip of her tongue against said elbow. I wouldn't exactly call it a full lick, but it was close enough.

Midlick, Marge said, "It's really . . . not that . . . hard to do."

We applauded gently. She curtsied.

The old man resumed reading. "She can only do the left one, though. The right one's a different story, but we're working on it."

I opened my wallet and removed the cash and extended it to the man. But he held up a hand. "No way, I was just kidding. Keep your money."

This was when I noticed the couple's saddlebags. They were green canvas, obviously homemade, and there were patches sewn on them. Dozens of patches. The embroidered badges read "Northern Tier Bicycle Route," "TransAmerica Bicycle Route," "Natchez Trace Trail," "Southern Tier Bicycle Route," "Pacific Coast Bicycle Route," "Lewis and Clark Bicycle Trail," "Atlantic Coast Bicycle Trail," "Bicycle Route 66," "KATY Trail Route," and "Appalachian Trail," with even more patches on the other bags.

"So where's home?" the old man asked.

"Florida."

He thumped his chest. "Abilene."

"Texas?"

"Kansas."

A few hours from my father's hometown.

I pointed. "I was admiring your patches."

"Yeah, we've been around." He touched a faded patch representing the Grand Canyon. "This was our first trip, back in '64 or '63. Happened right after my accident."

"We were so young," said his wife.

"Very young," he said. "We'd never been anywhere. After I got outta the hospital, I just said one day, 'You know what, Marge, we're gonna see the world.' So I quit my construction job and, by dog, that's what we did."

"It looks like you saw it a few times."

He smiled.

His wife, now in a full warrior pose, went on to tell us they had pedaled the entire width of the United States on three separate occasions. They'd hiked the Appalachian Trail four times—in both directions. They'd done parts of the Pacific Crest Trail. They had biked through Canada, Mexico, and a bunch of other places. Their stories were so grandiose they were difficult to believe. They looked like Ma and Pa Kettle. These were not the kind of people you would expect to gallivant across the United States on bikes. These were the kind of people you'd expect to conduct in-depth conversations on Medicare.

Together, they said they'd logged an estimated 150,000 miles on wheels since the early 1960s.

"But nothing, *nothing* was like the Grand Canyon," the old man said.

The woman did a forward bend. "It was spectacular."

"We were in our thirties. Before we went, Marge went to the thrift store, bought a bunch of canvas, and sewed our first backpacks. Back then they didn't sell backpacks like you got today. We wore regular old sneakers. We were totally unprepared. Hard to believe that we almost didn't go."

"Why not?"

"Because it scared us to death. People die in the canyon all the time. You didn't hike through the canyon in those days."

His wife asked, "Have you ever been to the Grand Canyon before?"

My wife and I nodded.

The old man shut the book. "People kept saying I shouldn't be doing this kinda thing, all this wilderness stuff, in my condition. Said I had no business being out there. People love to try to make you afraid, but that's only 'cause they're scared. But I don't listen to people. Fear never helped anyone."

The old woman noticed me rubbing my back. "Your back hurting, sweetie?"

"Old injury."

"What happened?"

"I had a disagreement with an F-150 on the interstate."

He resumed reading his book. "Marge can cure back pain."

"Oh no. That's all right, I'll be . . ."

But Marge was already manhandling me into what she called a cow's face pose. And because I was raised among polite, churchgoing people, I let Marge have her way with me. My wife used her state-of-the-art cell phone to document my foray into the wonderful world of yoga.

It should be noted that I've never successfully done anything yogic before other than the "corpse pose." I am about as flexible as municipal concrete. Still, it was novel to be lying on the grass near a two-hundred-year-old home doing ancient poses guided by a woman old enough to be my granny. Marge stood over me, guiding me in the finer points of stretching various lumbar muscles.

"Make sure you're squeezing your glutes, dear. That'll really help with the pain and help loosen your pelvic muscles."

I squeezed.

"Tighter, dear. Keep your core tight and those glutes flexed. Tuck your butt in a little more."

"That's right," said the math teacher. "Tuck it in. Tuck it *all* in."

After my yoga instruction, and approximately three thousand unapproved mobile phone photos, the elderly couple began adjusting the straps on their pannier bags and preparing for the day ahead. When the old man lumbered onto his machine, he made all the moans and winces appropriate for a man his age. It occurred to me that a long-distance trail must be a real feat for people in this stage of life. It was hard enough for me, and I'm not even old enough to qualify for AARP.

He snapped his helmet into place and donned a pair of aviator sunglasses. His helmet was one of those old-fashioned ones that looked like he was about to be shot out of a cannon.

He gave me a thumbs-up. "Be good," he said. "And if you can't be good, be good at it."

My old man used to say that.

That's when I noticed the man's right arm was mangled, beginning at the elbow. I hadn't seen it from my earlier views. He was missing a few fingers, and his remaining fingers were contorted. The angle of his elbow was unnatural, permanently bent. He saw me looking, but neither of us said anything. He'd probably answered more than enough questions about his arm.

He pointed and said, "You know your tires are going flat?"

I looked at my trike. He was right. One of the tires was losing air.

"I hate this stupid machine," I said.

He laughed. "Well, right now it's all you got, so don't hate it too much. It's what's gonna get you outta here."

He finished mounting his bike with extreme difficulty. Whatever accident he'd suffered had apparently affected the use of his leg too. His wife held the bike and assisted him. It took several minutes for the man to get situated. Before he left, we shook hands and he wished me luck. As they rode off, I could see the old man steering with only one hand resting on his handlebars, the other remaining firmly against his side. He pedaled with a lopsided efficiency, and his story made more sense to me.

I was brought back to the present moment by the sound of the math teacher's voice. "Hey, look," she said, flipping through a discarded paperback. "He left his book."

I became suddenly aware that my back pain had disappeared.

# 21

*And then I* got lost.

There is no way to know which exact US state I was in when it happened. The part of the trail I was riding jumps back and forth between West Virginia and Maryland. But the fact is, my wife and I became separated. Soon I was riding alone through the late afternoon sun, pedaling through a remote section of overgrown trail past roadblocks of impenetrable greenery, with no machete. I wasn't even sure I was on the trail or in some unidentified stretch of woods.

This was all my fault, of course. We had been riding at different paces all afternoon, and I kept lagging farther and farther behind because I was seated upon the Linda Blair of cycles. I finally told my wife not to wait for me and to ride at her own pace. I wanted her to enjoy herself on the trail and not to feel like she was always having to slow down for her little brother.

"Are you sure?" she had said. "I don't mind riding slow."

"Don't worry about me," I told her. "It's not like I'll get lost. This trail only goes two ways."

Famous last words.

Eventually the math teacher's legs carried her out of sight, and I was alone on the trail. It was no big deal at first. In fact, it was kind of nice being out there all by myself, communing with the birds and the sunbathing lizards. But then two hours turned into three. Three turned into four. Four into five. Our phones were not getting signals. And I had passed no other people on the overgrown path. Nothing but weeds surrounded me. The farther into the woods I pedaled, the more I recalled the wisdom found in the parable of Hansel and Gretel. Always leave a trail of Little Debbies.

There were no exits, no campgrounds, no evidence of civilization. No nothing. Just trees. I was pretty sure I wasn't on the trail at this point. Even now, I have no idea where I was or how I'd gotten there.

Oh, and my trike was officially coming apart. Until now, all my trike's mishaps had been merely dress rehearsal problems. I had stopped to air up my tires about a dozen times, but the slow leaks were not cooperating anymore. Soon I was riding on my rims through veritable mudholes, much like what I imagine the rain forest of the Congo Basin is like. I was moving about one mile per hour, plowing through tall grass and brown slime. I could feel my wheels sinking inches into the soft, mucky ground. As my solitude rounded the six-hour mark, I was starting to freak out. I couldn't get through this dense wilderness on my machine, and my wife could have already been in Virginia for all I knew.

Fear makes your thinking cloudy. You would think it

would work the opposite way. You'd think fear would make you sharp and alert. Instead, fear makes you drunk and confused. You start thinking stupidly, irrationally. It's only a matter of time before you start sucking your thumb.

I grew up with fear. Fear changed me. It changed the way my brain works; it changed my family. Needless to say, I was going through some major panic in the woods of West Virginia. Or was it Maryland?

Finally, I hit a piece of trail where my trike just gave up. Game over. The machinery quit and refused to go any farther. The harder I pedaled, the deeper I sank into the slough of despair. My gears quit working. My chain snagged. I was in muddy earth up to my hubs.

It was getting darker outside. The sounds of the woods grew more intense. Birds, crickets, the rushing Potomac, wind hissing through trees, and the sounds of mammal-like wildlife were enclosing me.

I checked my phone reception, but I had none. I attempted to push my trike forward, but it wouldn't move through the thicket and the muck. So I donned the horse collar and attempted pulling my cycle from the sinkhole. But even that wouldn't work.

Now it was black outside.

I clicked on my red hazard light, although I don't know why. Nobody would have seen the light through the miles of tightly packed weeds. And if I wasn't on the trail at all, the light was doubly worthless. I tried to remove my heavy backpack from my rack to lighten the trike's load, but my backpack was stuck. The straps were lodged in the gears. I tried to pry it free, but when the bag came loose, my momentum flung me backward, my boot heels slipped in the soup, and I landed butt-first in mud like something from an Abbott and Costello routine.

I rose to my feet and felt the weight of the wet earth clinging to the seat of my Wrangler cargo pants. I clicked on my headlamp, removed the bike from the mud, and surveyed the damage to my trike rims. The rims themselves were okay, but one tire was completely flat. Another tire had slipped off the rim.

I shouted into the night. "Jamie!"

Nothing.

"Hello?"

Echo.

Where was the trail? Where was my wife? Where was anyone? I'd been alone for hours. I had no way of knowing how far I was from the next trailhead, or the route itself, or the next town. Should I just keep walking? Should I stay here and try to fix my cycle in the dark?

I found a clearing where I wheeled my machine, and I collapsed in the weeds. I looked at my decrepit piece of three-wheeled affliction beneath the glow of my headlamp and wished I could throw it into the Potomac. The entire trike was covered in pancake mud, bow to stern. The inner tubes needed to be changed, or else I would never make it out of this place.

"Jamie!" I yelled again.

But I was only wasting energy. My shouts died before they ever made it above the suffocating treetops.

I sat beneath the dome of heaven, cross-legged in the grass, eating a protein stick and watching the stars. I leaned my head against a silver maple and ate a meager dinner of plywood-style beef. I had given up working on my trike for the time being because, unsurprisingly, I had only managed to make all mechanical problems worse, nearly ripping off my thumbnail in the process. When I had tried to unbend a steel gear sprocket with a flimsy screwdriver, I lost my grip on the tool and almost stabbed myself in the groin. I was lucky I didn't seriously hurt myself. A man could bleed to death out here and nobody would know.

The padre was right about the sky. The night looked like scattered crystals strewn across acres of purple velvet. I realize what I am about to say will sound like a cliché, but I had never seen anything like the sky that was above me. It was a showstopper.

There are approximately 170 galaxies observable from our universe. Some of these island universes have hundreds of trillions of stars. The Milky Way has about 400 billion. If you were to mush the stars together and then add all the dwarf galaxies, you'd get about a septillion stars. Still, most people have never seen the Milky Way. Half the globe lives in urbanized areas with so much sky glow that the stars are invisible. So you're not ready for it when you see it. You don't expect that a sky could look *that* impressive.

It does.

I think I was in my early thirties the last time I saw the Milky Way in all its glory. I remember that I was out on an evening walk in the dusk of West Florida with my wife, and it was the night before her father's funeral. My wife and I went out for a stroll that night after supper. We stopped every few feet so she could cry into my shoulder. It went like this for hours. Walk, stop, cry, repeat. And that's when we both noticed the cloudy formation in the sky, hanging above the Choctawhatchee Bay. It stunned us. It looked almost false. Like a silvery fog conjured up by artists with airbrushes. The whole time I was thinking, "If *that* exists, and I never see it, what *other* things exist that I don't know about?"

As I ate my beef stick, I was looking at the universe and wondering where I fit into all this. I was wondering why God allows good people to suffer and dictators to die of old age. I was wondering where people go when they die. I was wondering why I'm my own worst critic. I was wondering a lot of things. But mainly, I was wondering how I was going to get out of these woods.

When I finished supper, I decided to give my mechanical endeavors another attempt. I emptied my backpack into the grass and combed through its contents with both hands looking for the multi-tool and spare tubes. I ran through a few options in my mind and tried to remain rational. If I couldn't fix my trike, my only choice would be to abandon the cycle and keep going on foot. Was this smart? Or was it pure foolery? Would I be able to find the trail? Did I have a living will?

If I left my cycle, I'd have to leave most of my gear behind, since there was too much to carry. But hey, at least I'd be moving, which was better than just sitting here. Or was it? Would it be better to wait for someone to come along? Would anyone come along? What if I got lost out there? What if . . . ?

Enough.

After several minutes of working on my cycle, I started to feel better simply because I was doing something. Sometimes just doing something, anything, feels better than being uselessly still. I was out there for what felt like a decade screwing around with a dead tire and bent sprockets in the darkness. I was tired. I was mentally fatigued. It was not a good night. The only thing that could have made this moment worse was a . . .

*Sssssssssssssss.*

# 22

When I was sixteen, I attended the Rattlesnake Rodeo in Opp, Alabama, with my cousin Ed Lee and a few pals. I did this on a dare since my pals all knew I was mortified of snakes. Nothing good comes of dares. I don't know when dares began, or why. Neither can I figure out how dares are able to wield so much power over the young. I once saw my friend Todd Beasley dared to eat an earthworm. Todd did it. For years I've tried to figure out how Todd earned satisfaction from this feat. On one hand, Todd subjected his free will to the wiles of others who sought to make a fool of him. On the other hand, Todd ate a worm. Where was the payoff?

The Rattlesnake Rodeo turned out to be among the worst displays I'd ever seen. I watched a total lunatic wearing a cowboy hat and white tank top chase a rattlesnake in a small arena, capture it, milk its fangs into a glass, and chop its head off. Then the snake was marinated in exotic spices, cooked on a spit, and served on white Wonder bread. The smaller, less bony pieces were fried and sold like hotcakes to patrons of the rodeo. I was teased within an inch of my pride and double-dog dared to eat one of these sandwiches. I accepted my dare and ate rattlesnake. I would have rather eaten a worm.

For years, I believed that this was the worst snake experience one could possibly have. I simply could not imagine anything worse.

Until right now.

Somewhere in the deep woods of the mid-Atlantic, I saw an orangish snake with wild designs on its back moving toward me like it wanted to discuss Amway. At the time, I was working on my trike tire, stretching an inner tube onto the metal rim, positioned in a full crouch. The blood in my heart stopped. I watched the creature's luminescent body ease through the grass. The snake was only a few feet away, weaving in that sickly sideways-forward motion all snakes have perfected.

Thanks to all my wife's diligent research, I was a regular encyclopedia of snake factoids.

Copperheads are most active between late afternoon and evening when it is cool outside. Nighttime is when they hunt. They mostly eat rodents and other pests, but when they feel threatened, they will eat community-college graduates. Snake experts consider them to be one of the boldest snakes in the animal kingdom. They have no natural predators except owls. They rule the forest. They can jump, lunge upwards of seven feet, and even climb trees. They have reportedly been seen chasing their prey straight up the trunk of a sycamore if need be.

I remained motionless in my squatted pose, watching the snake's smooth skin beneath the cool blue LED glow coming from my headlight, and I prayed for a barn owl.

The snake was nothing if not purposeful. Its long body was efficient and graceful, with not a single economic movement wasted. With one gentle flick of its muscles, the thing nearly levitated through the grass, as if cutting through water. Of course, I wanted to scream and run, but this seemed about as smart as mailing the snake an invitation to my wake.

I thought about my hat. If it came down to it, maybe I could throw my hat on top of the snake, using it like a shield. It might buy me a few seconds at least. I was grasping at ideas. I attempted to steady my breathing, but my chest was thumping out disco bass lines, and I felt my whole body going numb from remaining so still for so long. Somehow, amazingly, I found the fortitude to keep looking directly at this creature. And in doing so, I surprised myself. The longer I looked at the snake, the less anxious I was feeling about it. I don't mean to suggest I wasn't totally wetting my pants here—I think we both know I was. But I was also growing a little stronger simply by not shrinking away. There was an important metaphor here, but I didn't have time to figure it out.

I watched the snake move left, pause, turn right, then pause again. I died a thousand deaths. Minutes passed. I had slowly worked my hat off, grasping it by the crown, ready for throwing. I rehearsed the move in my mind a few times. If I had to, I would toss it outward, brim down. I'd jump left. Maybe the lunging snake would miss its mark and I'd have time to run.

After a few more minutes, my right Achilles tendon was complaining, my knees were stoved up, and my thighs were cramping something awful. What I needed was to stand and stretch my legs. What I needed was to get out of this hunched stance and breathe. What I needed was beer.

The reptile made another agonizing loop around me so slowly that at times I felt like Roy Scheider during the final scenes of *Jaws*.

Then it made another loop, this time tighter.

And still, I did not move.

After what felt like forty-eight hours—but was probably more like five minutes—the snake decided I was either no threat or not worth the calories it would take to kill me. I watched as the thing made an about-face and moved away from me into the grass, slithering along the wagon ruts of the trail until its body disappeared beyond the glow of my headlamp and into the cobalt night.

I felt myself begin breathing again. Sensation returned to my limbs. I wanted to crumple into the grass and assume the fetal position, but I didn't. I stood. I stretched. I screwed my hat onto my head. Then, with remarkable calm, I changed my tire and managed to get my trike working. I finished the job in record time, as if guided by an unseen hand, and I got the Sam Hill out of there.

I pedaled forward through the night until I saw a blinking red light about a mile ahead of me, leading me to safety. Again, there's another metaphor in there somewhere, but I'll have to let you be the one to find it because I need to go change my trousers.

## 23

On October 25, 1783, Thomas Jefferson visited Harpers Ferry, West Virginia, on his way to Philadelphia with his daughter Patsy. One morning, he awoke before sunrise and went for a hike along a serene stretch of what is now known as the Appalachian Trail. He climbed a tall, flat shale rock, perched on a very high point of land overlooking miles of river and mountain summits. On his right was the Shenandoah, completing its route around granite sierras and limestone valleys, rushing into the gorge. On his left was the Potomac, lashing itself against boulders and mountainsides, smoothing each craggy stone standing in its way. The two rivers converged in a frothy fury while the morning sky above put on a spectacular show.

"The scene," Thomas Jefferson said, "is worth a voyage across the Atlantic."

He wasn't lying. It's stunning.

Jefferson Rock is a short hike from Harpers Ferry. You must follow the stone steps on High Street, beginning in Lower Town. Then you go past St. Peter's Catholic Church where you will find another set of stone steps leading upward. Your quadriceps will beg for mercy when the path takes you higher still, past the ruins of St. John Episcopal Church until, mercifully, you reach more steps.

As soon as you get to Jefferson Rock, you will be informed of two things: (1) you cannot stand on the rock, or (2) you will go to jail. The rock is unstable. Walking on, climbing, or ascending the rock is expressly prohibited. But the view is mostly the same as it was two hundred and thirty-odd years ago, and this is one of the few locations in America where such is the case.

My wife and I left our inn early that morning and stood at Jefferson Rock during sunup to watch the world below. The church spires reached their arms upward through the fuzzy trees, grasping at the pink sky above us.

"Dadgum," said my wife.

She's always had a way with words.

The town of Harpers Ferry is a high point of the C&O experience. If you ever have a chance to go, you should. What you will find here is a hamlet that was first settled in 1732 and looks pretty much the same as it did around the time of the Civil War. It has stunning river views, gracious mountains, and steep paved hills that will rip your calves in two. So bring the Advil.

The whole town is a national park, but it's also an operating tourist village. This means that people live here, work here, shop here, and sell funnel cakes here. In some places it feels like your prototypical American tourist trap. You see colorful neon signs in the windows of colonial shop fronts advertising things like cotton candy, CBD, Beanie Babies, deep-fried Oreos, and other tourist crapola. It's almost like the county fair, but with powdered wigs and knee breeches.

Along the giant slope leading into town sits a rainbow row of colorful homes that dot the mountainside like something from Europe. The styles of the homes tell the entire story of America. Architecture-wise, you have everything from Old English saltbox houses to arts-and-crafts homes to the weirdly decorated houses featuring Jerry Garcia–like characters meditating on their front porches.

You will at some point see a distant train carving its way across a faraway mountain shoulder, thereby completing the beautiful image before you. You can hear the diesel coach chugging around the tracks, and you will experience the uncontrollable urge to embrace your inner kid and say, "Look! Choo-choo!" Whereupon you might even buy a deep-fried Oreo.

In the nearby woods, the Appalachian Trail passes directly through Harpers Ferry. There is such a conjunction of history, nature, and American culture within Harpers Ferry that it would take the rest of this chapter to cover it all. And I would be happy to tell you all about it, except I can already see some of you nodding off.

After spending a restful day at our inn, my wife and I got ready to go out for dinner. Although getting "ready to go out for dinner" means different things to my wife than it does to me. So I left her to her cosmetic business while I walked into town to meet her at the restaurant. I descended the large hill leading into Lower Town—one of the most staggering hills I have ever encountered. One wrong step and you will tumble hundreds of feet downward into an ICU.

It was the shank of the evening when the hostess led me to my table. I sat alone while Mick Jagger sang "You Can't Always Get What You Want." I don't care for the song. It's depressing.

With sixty-one miles left, we were nearing the end of the trail. This meant I was done with weeds, mud, tents, the yeti, poison oak, and whatever else was out there. Above all, I did not ever want to see a slithering *Agkistrodon contortrix* again. I had not even told my wife about my snake experience. I could not have borne the string of jokes that would have followed.

I waited at my table while turning my beer bottle in its condensation ring. My legs were crossed, and Agatha Christie was in hand. I wore my dress Wranglers and a white button-down shirt that I'd purchased in Harpers Ferry proper for the criminal price of $98.95. Like I said, a tourist trap. But I felt great. There was something cold in my right hand, something fiction in my left, and Mick Jagger never sounded so hoarse.

I licked a thumb and turned a page. I was starting to wonder whodunit when I noticed a feminine figure enter the outdoor seating area. I put my book down and looked toward the approaching female.

This woman has always known how to make an entrance. She wore a blue knit blouse and jeans. She stood beneath the twinkling lights in the dining area, and Mick took another chorus.

I stood. Mostly because I didn't know what else to do.

She looked lovelier than I'd ever seen her. Trail Jamie had been replaced with Date Jamie. She was fresh and youthful, with a perpetual lightness to her features. And that girl-ish glow.

"Hi," said the algebraist.

"You look nice."

"Yeah, well . . ."

We sat.

"You really do look good," I said.

"You already said that, dork."

Ah, *amor*.

She glanced at the book on the table. "So how's the book?"

"The butler did it."

The town was humming with a sedate dinner crowd. It was a weekend, and we saw people from all walks of life. Old, young, married couples, huge families moving in clots down the streets.

The waitress came. "Another beer, sir?"

I shook my head. "No thanks. I have to drive my tri-cycle home."

"I'll take one," said Jamie.

Dinner was okay. Not great, but you can't always get what you want. I ordered a bleu cheese burger. My wife alternated between sweet potato fries, a crab cake, and her frosted beer glass. We ate in the blissful silence that only married couples know. People who have been married a while know how to go entire meals without saying anything more than "Supposed to rain tomorrow" or "Pass the salt." And they manage to communicate more love in those few words than the young can convey with fifty thousand.

Throughout supper, I kept thinking to myself about how we had pedaled almost 290 miles. That's not a huge number, but it's not nothing either. I could hardly believe it. Each mile was earned. Each rise and fall. Each hill. No, ours wasn't a great feat compared to what real athletes do. There are hikers who cover that kind of mileage before breakfast. But this accomplishment was ours.

"You really do look nice," I told the woman across from me.

"Will you quit it?"

All around us tourists, hikers, and day-trippers were wandering the street. Many of these were young people wearing heavy packs and trail boots and carrying hiking sticks. When they passed by our table, the foul scent of sweat followed in their wake. These were Appalachian Trail hikers. You will know them by their smell.

Harpers Ferry is not only a stop on the AT, but home to the headquarters of the Appalachian Trail Conference. The young people all looked pleasantly exhausted, carrying backpacks that were bigger than Plymouth Caravelles. By the time AT hikers have reached Harpers, they've already traveled 1,023 miles.

And here I was feeling proud of myself for 290 miles on wheels.

My wife killed her beer. "Can you believe we've come this far? I still can't believe we've almost done it."

"Me neither."

"Did you ever think we could do something like this?"

"I don't mean to be Johnny Raincloud here, but we're not done yet."

"Yeah, but two hundred and ninety miles."

It really did sound impressive.

We were interrupted by the sound of a female voice behind us.

"Hey, guys," the woman's voice said. I turned to see smiling eyes and a slender woman with bone-thin features. She was dressed in nice clothes—lace blouse and a pair of slacks.

"Sandy."

"Don't get up," she said. "I'm glad to see you guys made it in one piece. But I'm surprised you got your trike through all those weeds."

I said nothing.

"When did you get to Harpers?" said my wife.

"Been here since last night. I got to DC and Georgetown a few days ago. My daughter got tied up, so I hung around the city to see some of the history. Rode back here to wait for my daughter."

"So what's it like, finishing?" my wife asked.

Sandy's face answered before her words did. "Once you see that Washington Monument in the distance, you'll understand why you did it."

Just then a young woman came trotting up to Sandy.

The girl had honey-blond hair and wore a T-shirt with a Dartmouth logo on it. She was a younger version of the athletic woman before us, maybe midtwenties. She threw an arm around Sandy and called her Mom.

"This is my daughter, Andrea. She's my driver now. She's giving me the long ride back home tomorrow. Kid's trying to get me to hike the Appalachian Trail with her. She keeps begging. I hate it when they beg."

Andrea said, "I think it'd be fun."

"Maybe for the first mile it'd be fun," said Sandy.

There was admiration in Sandy's face when she looked at her daughter. Pride leaked out of the woman's eyes. I felt like I was intruding on a family moment.

"Your mom was the fastest biker out there on the trail," I said. "She outdid everyone."

"Oh, Mom's won big races," said the girl. "But she'd never tell anyone about it. She's very humble."

"They weren't *big* races," said Sandy.

The four of us talked about everything and nothing. Finally, we reached that awkward moment when you know it's time to end the conversation and go back to eating your sweet potato fries. We bid them goodbye. Sandy left with her daughter and left us with her favorite parting phrase. An Old English word rarely used anymore. An ancient word that comes from the phrase "God spede you," which literally translates into "Watch out for copperheads."

I would never see or hear from Sandy again. For all I know she will read this book someday by accident. I hope with all my heart she does. I hope she sees herself in the words I wrote and realizes how fervently I am hoping for her to see her grandbabies grow up. I hope she walks the Appalachian Trail with her daughter. I hope she proves every doctor wrong. I hope to see her again.

Jamie looked down and studied her beer for what felt like an infinity. "You think she'll be okay?"

I knew this question was deeper than it seemed. There was another annual medical checkup on our calendar in a few weeks. You do not relax after the doctor uses the c-word. Not ever.

"I hope she is okay," I said. It sounded like a weak response. But I kept thinking about how no matter what you hope for in this life, Mick Jagger's words will always remain so very true.

# 24

Somewhere in the far-flung wilds of West Virginia, deep within the dark recesses of the shadowed, murky, heartless, devilish woods, a miracle occurred. The trail opened up. The path ceased being a treacherous mess and was transformed primarily into crushed limestone and silt. This made for a much more level and smoother ride, for which we were grateful. The long miles of weeds and soup had at last been replaced with actual trail. I could have kissed the trail engineers. After I brained them, of course.

On the last day of our ride, we started meeting a lot of bikers on the towpath. Lots and lots of bikers. Other cyclists had been telling us that the trail gets crowded when you reach the C&O's terminus. Well, to say it was *crowded* only hints at the mass of people we encountered. At times we were caught in a caravan of maybe seventy or eighty people. Simply put, I was riding beneath a lot of butts.

This was when we realized how slowly we had been taking the two trails. You never get an accurate sense of how dawdling your pace is until you compare your daily mileage with other cyclists. We met one father-son duo from Minnesota who had completed the entire trail in two days. I met another woman, a police officer from San Francisco, who told me she once finished the trail in less time than that. I met a man from Boise, Idaho—also on a trike—who completed the trail in roughly seventy-two hours. This made me feel about as manly as a Malibu Barbie. It was clear: compared to other bikers, it had taken Jamie and me longer to finish the trail than it takes most people to finish a PhD.

But we had done it, and nobody can take that away from us.

By the time we reached Georgetown, we were pedaling much faster. I'm not sure why; maybe we were trying to impress all the bikers around us. Maybe we were caught in the flow of cycling traffic, a phenomenon known as "race pace." Or maybe the excitement of finishing was simply too much to rein our emotions inward. My wife was pedaling so fast I could hardly keep up, and I was adrift in a sea of glutes.

When we arrived at Rock Creek Parkway, we were officially out of the woods. We took Rock Creek Trail and followed a clot of bikers toward Washington's Union Station. The path hugged the Potomac, our constant traveling companion, and the river was in good spirits that day. The trail then carried us through the outskirts of an urban environment complete with traffic, vagrants, and of course, a Target. It was a shock to the system to leave the woods and find yourself in a city of nearly 700,000 people driving SUVs equipped with roaring 5.3-liter engines. It was an assault on the senses. It was frightening.

Then we saw it.

We braked and dismounted.

The first major landmark you see when you arrive at the National Mall from the trail is the Lincoln Memorial, standing in the distance like a relic from another age. You're not ready for it. Nobody is. You've known it was coming for miles, but you're still not ready because you never expect things to end. Then again, endings are what make things good. Even bad things become much better once the end occurs. Take, for example, this book.

Cyclists were shedding helmets, sweaty hair matted to their foreheads. We saw people leaping off their saddles to pose for photos with loved ones. We saw young couples kissing and others locked in tight embraces. It was a lot like the displays of emotion we'd seen when we finished the GAP trail, only this was more intense. I watched one cycling couple, a young man and young woman, hold each other and sway, staring at the Lincoln Monument, wiping their eyes with their shirtsleeves. I saw a father and his young son squeezing each other and twirling.

"It's over," said my wife.

"Yeah."

We were breathing heavily, staring at the Lincoln Monument's white Greek Doric temple with its thirty-six fluted Yule marble columns. Beyond the memorial stands the 555-foot Washington Monument, stabbing into the sky like an exclamation point. This too is worth a voyage across the Atlantic.

The entire town looked photographic to our trail-weary

eyes. The Capital City was bathed in the hues of an approaching dusk, and if there has ever been a prettier day, it exists only in a Disney-animated feature film.

We crawled back onto our horses and followed Jefferson Drive past the Smithsonian Museums. We took Third Street past the east wing of the National Art Gallery and then hopped onto Louisiana Street where we were granted a stunning view of the ivory Capitol dome. There, I was nearly run over by a cabdriver with homicidal tendencies, two transit buses, and a man riding a Vespa scooter bearing a cardboard protest sign littered with swear words about tax reform. Welcome to Washington.

But even these things couldn't faze me. Nothing could. We were here. This was the end. The wheels on my trike were turning crookedly like lopsided, mutant donuts. My derailleur was clicking like Pat Sajak's game show wheel. But as I say, none of this mattered anymore. It was over. Praise the Lord and pass the tacos.

We stopped at a Mexican food truck with a long line of customers stringing backward toward the Smithsonian Museum of Natural History. We got our food and ate on the steps of the Lincoln Memorial with salsa spilling down our chins and onto our sweat-laden shirts. Crowds were wandering upon the grandiose staircase of the sixteenth president. Random children kept asking about my trike. "I've never seen anything so weird." "What a funky little bike." "Why you have to ride a bike like that? Are you injured?" "That lady over there says you're afraid of clowns. Is that true?"

Our bodies were covered in salt crystals from evaporated perspiration. And we had fallen mute, watching the area overflow with toddlers playing and families sprawling on picnic blankets. There were buskers strumming, dogs barking, food vendors, sounds of laughter. Compared to the trail, this felt like being at the county fair. And I could not seem to find words to describe what I was feeling. We were finished.

And yet I didn't feel like we'd done anything remarkable.

I suppose I had expected to feel the kind of elation that comes from a grand accomplishment, but it wasn't like that. After 350 miles there were no cinematic moments. That's not how life works. Mountaintop experiences only happen in books and on Netflix. But my life isn't a book. It's ordinary. And even though I want it to be more sometimes, it's not. There are no film scores, no lighting effects, no A-list actors with high cheekbones. There is only us. There is only now.

Our watery smiles were growing hard to contain. People traipsed past us on the steps of the memorial, and we found ourselves caught in a communal glow. We didn't hug. We didn't kiss. We simply sat on the steps facing each other, holding hands. Her in her green hat. Me in my ridiculous ten-gallon lid.

"We did it," said Jamie.

"Sorta feels weird."

"No more pedaling."

"I am going to push my trike off a bridge."

We were silent again.

"What're you thinking?" the math teacher finally said.

I smiled.

What was I thinking? I wasn't sure, exactly. Maybe I was thinking about how a pandemic was no closer to being over than it had been before we'd left. Or perhaps I was thinking about how I was still very much unemployed.

Then I started thinking about how one of the main features of doing the trail comes afterward, during the rediscovering of things you temporarily left behind. All the things you took for granted. Radio ball games at dusk. Evenings on the porch. Sleeping in. Feeding your dogs scraps from the table. Waking up during the still hours of the morning and admiring the bone structure of a woman who has shared a couple decades of your life. Eating pizza on the tailgate at dusk to celebrate your wife's new math certification. I was ready to get back to those things again. I thought about many things. But most of all, I was thinking about how having Jamie Martin Dietrich beside me just feels good.

"I don't know," I said. "What about you? What're you thinking?"

She put an arm around my shoulder. "I'm thinking I don't ever want to eat another beef stick again."

Hear, hear.

# Epilogue

*After all these years, I see that I was*
*mistaken about Eve in the beginning;*
*it is better to live outside the Garden*
*with her than inside it without her.*

—SAMUEL CLEMENS

*There was a* sickly medical smell in the air. The hospital exam room is not my favorite place on earth. The mud-gray walls made my stomach churn. The persistent hum of air conditioners and overhead fluorescent lighting made me slightly nauseous. My wife sat on an exam table wearing a backless gown. The bruises on her thigh, a parting gift from her fall in the Keystone State, had faded. The scrapes on her forearm were completely healed. She still had numb hands from her cyclist's palsy.

It seemed like light years ago that we had completed the

two trails. I sat in a chair in the corner of the doctor's exam room: the husband chair. My knees were bouncing the way they do whenever I have to go to the bathroom or when I get nervous. Or in this case: both.

Nurses kept tapping on the door and telling us that the doctor would be right in. "Shouldn't take long," they would say.

This was supposed to be a routine checkup. But when we had arrived that morning, the nurse tech who did the ultrasound waved the transducer over my wife's midsection and grimaced. "Uh-oh," she'd said.

"What's *uh-oh?*" I said.

The woman pointed out a possible mass on the screen. "I don't like this."

"What do you mean?" said my wife.

"We're gonna need to check this out," the woman said gravely.

We felt our chests tighten, and old anxieties returned.

The powers that be sent us upstairs to another doctor. Then downstairs again. We had spent all morning between waiting rooms, hoping for an opening. It was late afternoon now. It had been a long day of reading through *Highlights* magazines and outdated *Guideposts* articles about Trisha Yearwood's ongoing crusade to consume more dietary fiber.

They let me in the exam room with Jamie, which was nice. They didn't always do that. When the doctor entered, he was a smallish man with silver hair and a lowland drawl that was pure South Carolina. He could probably sense our fretfulness when he greeted us.

Once again, I wanted to ralph. I just knew what he was going to say before his mouth opened. *We need more tests.* I was braced for it. That's what they said last time. That's what they always say. This is what all men and women with multiple letters behind their names tell you. It's their mantra. They rarely give you an all clear. You could wander into any medical office, for any reason, including to read the gas meter, and they would recommend *more tests.*

The doc, however, didn't say that. In fact, he didn't say much at all. Instead, he sat on a rolling stool, which put him at eye level with my wife's knees. He turned and spoke to a nurse quietly.

"Sandy," he said, "show this man what's behind door number three."

Sandy. That was her name. Don't tell me God doesn't dabble in stand-up comedy.

A young blonde in scrubs showed me to the corner of the exam room where a privacy curtain was hanging. "Step behind the curtain, please, sir."

I did as I was told.

"Why am I standing behind a curtain?" I asked.

The doctor laughed. "Because you've been a very bad boy."

The nurse pulled the curtain closed, and I sat in yet another husband chair, where I assume all husbands sit when doctors examine their wives' groinal regions. I was separated from my wife by a thin blue curtain with angel cows printed on it. I studied these celestial bovines that were apparently flying upward to the hereafter and listened to the doctor speak to my wife in a calm voice. He had a great bedside manner, a rarity in the medical world.

"Is that too uncomfortable, ma'am?"

Jamie drew in a sharp breath. "Well, your hands are like ice cubes. So yeah, I'd say it's a little uncomfortable."

The nurse popped into my shower stall to keep me informed. She whispered, "He's just checking her ovaries right now."

"Ovaries. Right."

"How does that feel?" the doctor asked.

"It hurts," said my wife.

The nurse smiled and repeated the slogan that must be part of the Hippocratic Oath. "Shouldn't take long."

I could hear my wife sucking more air through her teeth. I heard the squeak of vinyl upholstery. The crinkle of the wax paper covering the exam table—what is that paper for anyway?

"Sorry, Mrs. Dietrich," the doc said. "I know this is not fun. Almost done."

All I could do was stare at the heavenly Jersey cows with their little cherub wings and happy faces. The little cows reminded me of how my father used to always say "when pigs fly" whenever something seemed impossible. My father wasn't always a tragic man. At one time he had been a hopeful kid, like anyone else, a kid with real dreams. But his family handed him a blue-collar belief system that could be summed up as "Life sucks and then you die." My father was a man who was taught not to expect much out of life, and therefore he was rarely disappointed.

My people were dark people, a melancholy people. Optimism was not our go-to philosophy. We were a glass-half-empty clan, and when things got really bad, we believed our glasses were half-empty with fertilizer. There in that husband chair, I told myself I wasn't going to be that way. Not anymore. I have not survived suicide, poverty, and a youth devoid of education only to become someone who rolls over and gives up in the face of trials. I have looked a copperhead in the face and lived to tell the story, thank you very much. I choose to believe that the Almighty is the kind of guy who will make his pallet in hell alongside me.

"Almost through," the doc said.

I heard my wife wince again.

Finally, I heard the snap of a plastic glove.

The bovid mammal curtain was slung open like a reenactment of the shower scene from *Psycho*. And I was back in the game.

The doctor was not looking at the math teacher, nor at me. The older man was staring at a clipboard in his lap, flipping pages. I could feel my pulse in my ears.

My wife took my hand.

"Well, Mrs. Dietrich . . . ," he said with a sigh.

Time and space slowed to an imperceptible crawl. I felt my fingers pop beneath her squeeze. Whatever he said, whatever happened, it was going to be okay. I made that decision for myself right there. I only hoped I could back it up.

"I've just examined your ovaries, and to be quite honest . . ." He looked at me and then back to her. A warm grin worked its way onto his face. I didn't even need to hear him speak after that. I just knew.

"Mrs. Dietrich, you look great. I don't see any problems. I'm giving you an all clear."

The math teacher did not react at first. I watched as her lower lip quivered. And it seemed like I was miles above the world, floating somewhere in the corner of the room. I saw the medical man stand and leave the room to give us a few moments of privacy.

Before he left, he winked at me and said, "Go hug your wife."

The door shut. We were alone. Neither of us moved for a few moments. The room was mostly quiet. The AC compressor kicked on. The overhead lights buzzed. Jamie slowly rose from the deli-counter wax paper, arms held outward like a tired toddler ready for a nap. We stood in one place doing the senior-prom-dance hug. The empty exam room took on a brighter hue, much like the sunshine that hangs over the Alleghenies during the height of summer. I felt her chest rise and fall in little gasps. I heard her sniffle. I cried with her.

Eventually, the math teacher released me. Her chocolate eyes were ringed with pink circles, and her cheeks were slick with water. Her nose was stuffy. She smiled. Without saying a word, she presented her hand in a sign language gesture. Index, pinky, and thumb extended. Middle fingers down.

And I could not have said it better myself.

# Acknowledgments

*As ever, I* am much indebted to many people for their expert help and guidance in writing this book and for just generally helping me not to sound like a complete hick. I want to thank the fine people at the GAP Conservancy for answering questions and for providing trail goers with *TrailGuide: The Official Guide to Traveling the C&O Canal Towpath and Great Allegheny Passage*, where much of the information in this book came from. Any mistakes in this book are probably their fault.

I also want to extend a heartfelt thanks to the scores of local volunteers who live in or near trail towns and have assumed the sole responsibility of maintaining 150 miles of mountain trail, which requires a lot of Weed Eater line.

Thank you to the Mountain Maryland Trails, the Somerset County Recreation and Trails Association, the Yough River Trail Council, the Whitsett-Fayette Yough Trail Chapter, the Westmoreland Yough Trail Chapter, the Mon/

Yough Trail Council, the McKeesport Trail Commission, the Steel Valley Trail Council, and Friends of the Riverfront.

And when it comes to the C&O Towpath, I want to thank Mike High for his wonderful book, *The C&O Canal Companion*, without which I would have had no earthly idea what in the heck I was looking at while on the trail.

Finally, thank you to the 20,000 uncommon men and women who passionately administer, protect, and manage our country's national parks. National parks truly are one of the greatest ideas America ever had.

# Notes

## Chapter 1

4   *There had been a 54 percent* . . . : Michael S. Pollard, Joan
    S. Tucker, and Harold D. Green Jr., "Changes in Adult
    Alcohol Use and Consequences during the COVID-19
    Pandemic in the US," *JAMA Network* 3, no. 9 (September
    2020), doi:10.1001/jamanetworkopen.2020.22942.

## Chapter 2

13   *The excited response was* . . . : Paul G. Wiegman, "Great
     Allegheny Passage: Turning a Dream into the Nation's
     Greatest Bike Trail," *Pittsburgh Quarterly*, August 25, 2008,
     https://pittsburghquarterly.com/articles/great-allegheny
     -passage/.

16   *Only a year before we would* . . . : Gina Cook, "Woman Dies
     after Hiking on Billy Goat Trail during Extreme Heat," NBC
     Washington, July 21, 2019, https://www.nbcwashington.com
     /news/local/woman-dies-from-heat-related-illness-after-hiking
     -in-great-falls/135570/.

16   *A man in his sixties* . . . : Dave McMillion, "Pa. Bicyclist Dies

after Falling into Canal Lock near Shepherdstown," Herald Mail Media, May 26, 2019, https://www.heraldmailmedia .com/news/breaking/pa-bicyclist-dies-after-falling-into-canal -lock-near-shepherdstown/article_9a60176d-3e44-58e7-891d -e51ea42c203f.html.

16  A *fifty-six-year-old guy* . . . : "Bicyclist Killed by Falling Tree in Storm on C&O Canal Towpath," WJLA Maryland, July 4, 2011, https://wjla.com/news/local/bicyclist-killed-by -falling-tree-in-storm-on-c-o-canal-towpath-63159.

17  *Not long before we would take the trail* . . . : "Police Release Detailed Description of Bike Trail Attacker," *Pittsburgh Post-Gazette*, September 25, 2019, https://www.post-gazette .com/local/south/2019/09/25/great-allegheny-passage-bike -trail-attack-rapist-description-police-bicyclist/stories /201909250174.

17  *I learned that Pennsylvania* . . . : Marcus Schneck, "Is Bigfoot in Pennsylvania? Sightings Reported for More Than 150 Years: Monsters of Pennsylvania," Penn Live, updated January 5, 2019, https://www.pennlive.com/life/2019/06 /where-are-pennsylvanias-bigfoot-hotspots.html.

17  *The state ranks in the top* . . . : Marcus Schneck, "Have You Seen Bigfoot? More Than 1,300 Sightings Have Been Reported in Pa.," Penn Live, updated May 9, 2019, https:// www.pennlive.com/life/2019/05/pennsylvania-third-best -state-for-spotting-bigfoot-says-report-database.html.

18  *Rats carry hantavirus pulmonary* . . . : Bruce Barcott, "The Story behind the Hantavirus Outbreak at Yosemite," *Outside* (online), December 18, 2012, https://www.outsideonline .com/1930876/death-yosemite-story-behind-last-summers -hantavirus-outbreak.

18  *That same year, a man* . . . : Frank Eltman, "LI Professor Contracts Hantavirus in Adirondacks," NBC New York,

October 12, 2012, https://www.nbcnewyork.com/news
/local/long-island-case-of-hantavirus-in-adirondacks
-stonybrook/1964231/.

## Chapter 3

20  *Hanna Eskland was four years . . .* : "Copperhead Bites
4-Year-Old," Connection Newspapers, June 26, 2002,
http://www.connectionnewspapers.com/news/2002/jun/26
/copperhead-bites-4-year-old/.

20  *Amazingly, a passerby came . . .* : "Copperhead Bites
Dangerous, Not Deadly," Connection Newspapers, July 1,
2002, http://www.connectionnewspapers.com/news/2002
/jul/01/copperhead-bites-dangerous-not-deadly/.

## Chapter 9

73  *The Alleghenies had become so associated . . .* : "Almost an
Alleghanian: Or How N-YHS Tried to Change the Nation's
Name to the United States of Alleghania," New-York
Historical Society Museum and Library, January 30, 2013,
http://blog.nyhistory.org/almost-an-alleghanian-the-new-
york-historical-societys-bid-to-change-the-nations-name-to-
the-united-states-of-allegania/.

73  *Irving's second choice for a . . .* : Wikipedia, s.v. "Allegheny
Mountains," last updated on April 15, 2022, https://
en.wikipedia.org/wiki/Allegheny_Mountains.

74  *The Alleghenies and Appalachians . . .* : Wikipedia, s.v.
"Appalachian Mountains," last updated on April 19, 2022,
https://en.wikipedia.org/wiki/Appalachian_Mountains.

75  *Yellow birches line your path . . .* : "List of Western PA
Natives," Audubon Society of Western Pennsylvania,
http://www.aswp.org/pages/list-natives.

## Chapter 17

150 *Enter Supreme Court Justice* . . . : Wikipedia, s.v. "Chesapeake and Ohio Canal National Historical Park," last updated on February 12, 2022, https://en.wikipedia.org /wiki/Chesapeake_and_Ohio_Canal_National_Historical _Park.

# Will the Circle Be Unbroken?

## A Memoir of Learning to Believe You're Gonna Be Okay

*Sean of the South, Sean Dietrich*

From celebrated storyteller "Sean of the South" comes an unforgettable memoir of love, loss, the friction of family memories, and the unlikely hope that you're gonna be alright.

Sean Dietrich was twelve years old when he scattered his father's ashes from the mountain range. His father was a man who lived for baseball, a steel worker with a ready wink, who once scaled a fifty-foot tree just to hang a tire swing for his son. He was also the stranger who tried to kidnap and kill Sean's mother before pulling the trigger on himself. He was a childhood hero, now reduced to a man in a box.

*Will the Circle Be Unbroken?* is the story of what happens after the unthinkable, and the journey we all must make in finding the courage to stop the cycles of the past from laying claim to our future.

Sean was a seventh-grade drop-out, a dishwasher then a construction worker to help his mother and sister scrape by, and a self-described "nobody with a sad story behind him." Yet he cannot deny the glimmers of life's goodness even amid its rough edges. Such goodness becomes even harder to deny when Sean meets the love of his life at a fried chicken church potluck, and harder still when his lifelong love of storytelling leads him to stages across the southeast, where he is known and loved as "Sean of the South."

A story that will stay with you long after the final page, *Will the Circle Be Unbroken?* testifies to the strength that lives within us all to make our peace with the past and look to the future with renewed hope and wonder.

*Available in stores and online!*

ZONDERVAN®
.com